IT DEPENDS: A POET'S NOTEBOOK

Also by Eugenio Montale

New Poems
Selected Poems
Xenia, G. Singh, trans.*

* Black Sparrow Press

EUGENIO MONTALE

IT DEPENDS:
A POET'S NOTEBOOK

(Quaderno di quattro anni)

TRANSLATED AND INTRODUCED BY
G. SINGH

A NEW DIRECTIONS BOOK

ACKNOWLEDGMENTS
The publisher and editor would like to thank both the New York
and Milan offices of Arnoldo Mondadori Editore for their coopera-
tion in making this bilingual edition possible. The Italian text is
included by permission, all rights reserved by Arnoldo Mondadori
Editore.

Some of the translations included in this volume have previously
appeared in *London Magazine.*

Although *Quaderno di quattro anni* literally means "A Notebook
of Four Years," the translator and publisher have exercised their
license in taking the title of the English language edition from the
poem "Literary Histories."

Manufactured in the United States of America
First published clothbound and as New Directions Paperbook 507
in 1980
Published simultaneously in Canada by George J. McLeod, Ltd.,
Toronto

Library of Congress Cataloging in Publication Data

Montale, Eugenio, 1896-
    It depends—Quaderno di quattro anni.
    (A New Directions Book)
    I. Title.
PQ4829.0565Q313   1980   851'.912   80-16629
ISBN 0-8112-0773-0
ISBN 0-8112-0774-9 (pbk.)

New Directions Books are published by James Laughlin
by New Directions Publishing Corporation,
80 Eighth Avenue, New York 10011

CONTENTS

INTRODUCTION

by G. Singh

In his introductory note to what was to be his last book, *Winter Words* (in fact, it appeared just after his death), Thomas Hardy observed: "So far as I am aware, I happen to be the only English poet who has brought out a new volume of his verse on his (eighty-eighth) birthday, whatever may have been the case with the ancient Greeks, for it must be remembered that poets did not die young in those days." Eugenio Montale, who has translated one of Hardy's most delicate lyrics "The Garden Seat," and whose own *It Depends: A Poet's Notebook* (*Quaderno di quattro anni*) came out in his eighty-second year, belongs to that small group of twentieth-century poets who, like Hardy and Pound (*Drafts and Fragments*, 1970), published a volume of verse in their eighties—poets who, as Hardy says of the ancient Greeks, "burnt brightlier towards their setting-day" ("An Ancient to Ancients," *Late Lyrics and Earlier*).

But if Montale's creative flame burns indefatigably, in spite of age, it does so because he neither rests on past laurels—his achievements in terms of linguistic, stylistic, and technical innovations—nor does he make a passive or mechanical use of his powers acquired over more than half a century of creative activity. His inventive and exploratory instinct is as fresh as ever so that everything he writes strikes one as being at once new and characteristic. His mastery over himself and his material comes out especially in the ease and self-assurance with which he faces the challenge of handling themes and concepts he hasn't dealt with before. This makes him take nothing for granted—not even his own skill. Of course, as has been the case with almost all the poetry he has written since *La bufera e altro*, Montale's poetic involvement has been increasingly with prosaic truths, sardonic wit, and ironical comments concerning the contemporary world of which he is such a shrewd and perceptive observer. He doesn't look upon the world as an outsider, but as one who, to quote Hazlitt, is *in* it, not *of* it. That is why Montale's use of moral and intellectual irony is so effective in illustrating his involvement in as well as his detachment from the world he is probing into. In a word irony provides him with a means of distancing what he is dealing with.

However, for all the changes or developments Montale's later poetry might have undergone, there is still a significant and unmistakable link between his later and his earlier poetry—a link in the form of echoes and reminiscences from, as well as allusions to, his earlier poetry, which are deeply embedded in *It Depends*. One can say that Montale's past never appears to be altogether past, nor is his present the less present for having its roots in the past. Otherwise how to explain the double-edged pathos underlying such poems as "Intellectual Education," "In

My Early Years," "To Pio Rajna," "That Which Remains (If It Does)," "The Woman of the Lighthouse," "From the Other Bank," "Aspasia," and "Beyond the Small Enclosure of Wrought Iron"—poems which, insofar as they bridge the gulf between the past and the present, give a unique dimension to Montale's later poetry? For instance, the transition from youth (when "the most violent wind was still a caress," in "Intellectual Education") to old age is aptly enacted by the sea's "cruel assaults on the pier" and by the fact that it is "no longer tasseled with sails"—details that depict the poet's early world possessed and lost and repossessed, something more real and more living than "the Chimeras, the ghosts of a preworld." For in the very act of repossessing the past, memory not only remolds what is lost, but puts an altogether different valuation on it. Thus, of the little dog Galiffa of "In My Early Years," what remains in memory is merely "that leap and that yelp" with which he used to reach Montale "with great bounds/up the winding stairs," the poet adding with a characteristic blend of irony and pathos, "nor does much more remain of great loves." That is why the son of the bailiff who gave Galiffa its name is "less alive than the dog" in the poet's insomnia.

Montale's ability to probe into the nature of memory and how it works is that of a poet-cum-psychologist. "He/who digs into the past," he tells us in "To Pio Rajna," "would know/that barely a millionth of a second/divides the past from the future," and his own poetry bears testimony to that. Only a millionth of a second may divide the past from the future, but what divides "a chronological death" from real death is much more—something that cannot be measured in terms of time. Hence the old illiterate bearded maidservant is remembered more than anything or anybody else, even though she died long ago—so long indeed that "if she were to enter my room now she would be/one hundred and thirty and I would cry with fright" ("That Which Remains [If It Does]"). While in Montale's world, which his poetry cannot but reflect, the past is inseparably linked with the present, in terms of art and technique his past is not so much a legacy as a burden to him, a burden from which, through one stage of development after another, he has always tried to free himself. For instance, in "Half a Century Ago," while referring to an admirer's congratulations to him on the fiftieth anniversary of the publication of *Ossi di seppia* Montale says: "I would like to tell him to go to the devil./I don't like being nailed down to history/for four verses or little more."

It is not so much on the technical or artistic planes, nor even on the thematic one, as on the plane of the exploration of one's own identity that the link with the past is relevant—an exploration that in Montale's case started with *Ossi di seppia* (particularly with such poems as "My Life, I Don't Ask For Set Features"). In a number of poems in this latest collection, the exploration, definition, and pinpointing of certain facets of the poet's personal identity continue, using strikingly new images, new criteria, and a new code of values and concepts. In fact, the poet's own sense of personal identity changes with the passage of time and in the light of what his new experiences, observations, and reflections have brought him. No wonder he can say (in "Murder is not my Strong Point"):

> I've now discovered that living
> is not a question of dignity
> or of any other moral category.
> It doesn't depend, never did
> depend on us. Dependence
> may sometimes make us feel
> elated, it never cheers us up.

And yet, Montale observes, "Our personal identity doesn't always/or almost never coincides with time/ which can be measured with the instruments we have" ("The Mirages"). Hence the more conscious the poet is of his own identity through the passage of time as well as through the mutations of chance and circumstance, the more jealously he guards it— a theme treated in "Protect Me," one of the most personal poems in *It Depends*.

In Montale's development away from *La bufera e altro* the keynote has always been a transition from the lyrical to the ironic, from the symbolic to the matter-of-fact, from the personal to the impersonal, and this even in the treatment of a theme so dear to him as the one in which he defines his sense of personal identity. That is why from *Satura* onwards, wit, irony, and satire have increasingly characterized Montale's thought, expression, and sensibility, calling into play all his powers as poet, man, and thinker.

But irony is seldom used by Montale merely as a literary device; it is pregnant both with thought and sentiment which another poet might have tackled in a lyric or philosophic vein. For example, in "Jehovah's Witnesses," while dealing with the theme of death, he observes, "If the thought of death was sad,/the thought that All will last/is the most frightening"; in "Harmony," on the other hand, the poet tells the imaginary character Adelheit that "Harmony belongs to the chosen/but on condition that they're unaware of it"; in "The Inhuman," Montale tells his dead wife, "You left in a hurry thinking/that he who makes the first move/gets the best place. But what place/and where?"—a typically Montalian manner of treating semi-facetiously a theme like that of the hereafter. And in "Locuta Lutetia" a gaunt old woman observes that if the world is going to the dogs it is not only the fault of men, and she does so while "sipping a crushed-ice drink through/a straw at the Café de Paris." "I don't know who she was," Montale tells us, but "At times/Genius is almost a paltry thing,/a bout of coughing."

The intimate union between the poet and the journalist in Montale is more or less the underlying principle behind all his verse from *Xenia* onwards; it is particularly active in *It Depends* in which wit, irony, and sarcasm, while being used for a critical as well as a creative end, give a new edge and a new timbre to his poetic diction. His sense of contemporaneity itself is tied up with the way he employs wit and irony, in order to diagnose the myths and assumptions, the values and dogmas of his age. And if his view of the modern world and civilization is, on the whole, drastically negative, it nonetheless makes for a new kind of poetry. In "Soliloquy," while musing on the absence of great men in the present, Montale tells us that "what remains of them/ is their unreliable biographies"—adding parenthetically, "certainly no one will write mine"—biographies full of such details as "the palace where Tristan/was composed," "the hole where Henry James/ tasted *crêpes suzette*," "the house where for years/ lived a famous pederast who was murdered elsewhere." But the very fact that such details alone can "satiate the ravenous/jaws of the future" is a sardonic comment on the present no less than on the future.

Parody and sarcasm serve Montale in his criticism of the *Zeitgeist* just as much as wit and irony do—criticism which, for all its negative drift, has an implicitly positive aim. "Easter Sunday Evening" tells us, while offering us Montale's parody of twentieth-century religion, that "Christ on the cross was singing/like a tenor overcome by/a sudden attack of pop colic./A short while before he had been tempted/by the devil in the guise of a naked woman./This is twentieth-century religion." Parody also serves Montale as a means of turning upside down the scale of values, and presenting what is ideal or sublime in terms of a humdrum reality. In other words, he probes into the nature of things both as a poet and as a journalist, creating novel effects. In "The Evening Hours," while assessing the dividing line between news and history, he tells us: "We shall have to wait quite a while/before the news is camouflaged as history."

In *It Depends*, there is no subject, however lofty or commonplace, which doesn't lend itself to the new mode, idiom, and technique through which Montale conveys his "criticism of life," thereby coming closer than ever before to abrogating the boundary line between prose and poetry, journalism and literature. This, however, doesn't mean that Montale's later poetry is altogether cerebral. Moreover, whatever is cerebral about it is not so much a matter of the absence of lyricism or imaginative content as of the way they are transformed into irony and sarcasm. For example, in "The Animals," while referring to those species of animals which are on the verge of extinction, Montale tells us that they "arouse consternation in those who suspect/that their Father has lost the mold." And the cause of their extinction is not men or climates, but the fact that "He/who made them thought they were useless/to the unhappiest of his products: us." In "Once," while musing on "hypothetical atlases/of lives without beaks, without feathers,/irretrievably lost through the millennia,/insects, reptiles, fish,"

Montale hints at the disappearance of man as well, which "fits in perfectly with the total/with its quite different involvements, and blind/as to who might have means of motion/or reflection." This is Montale's way of epitomizing the theory which Hardy expounded in *The Dynasts* concerning the working of "that immense unweeting Mind . . ./far above forethinking . . ./That knows not what It knows, yet works therewith" (Part First, Act V, Scene iv). Elsewhere, in "Big Bang or Something Else," Montale finds it strange that the universe should have been born either as a result of an explosion or derived from "the swarming of a stagnation"; and even stranger that it should have issued "from the magic rod/of a god with frighteningly/anthropomorphic features." As to the life hereafter, or the question of survival in the form of a personal identity, Montale treats this subject too (in "We'll Meet Again") in a characteristically reductive way, thereby achieving the effect of unobtrusive poignancy mingled with wit: "Up there/down there we won't even find/ Nothingness and it's no small thing./We shall have neither ether nor fire."

If Montale uses a witty, ironic, or sarcastic style to convey his musings on, or dabblings in metaphysics, theology, or philosophy, he uses it no less, and no less successfully, in his personal poems where the various facets of his own personality or of that of his wife Mosca—the protagonist of *Xenia*— are commented on at once wittily and poetically. In "When I Began to Paint," while referring to Mosca's illness, Montale asks her how she is: "rotten you said but no doubt there is somebody worse off." In "Solitude," one of his most poignant and impersonally personal poems, Montale tells us how the pigeons that peck at crumbs on his windowsill are agitated if he goes away for a couple of days, and how order is restored by an extra ration of crumbs when he comes back. But the blackbird that goes to and fro between the old man living opposite and Montale is disappointed: "My family," says Montale, "is reduced/to so little. And some have one/or more, alas what a waste!" In such a poem pathos masquerades as irony, and irony itself serves to distance and impersonalize what is personal. In "The Hiding Places," having mislaid Mosca's photograph—"I don't know where I might have hidden/your photograph. Had it come to light/it would have been a nuisance"—all Montale remembers about her is a cloud of her hair and "those innocent eyes/which contained everything and even more." In other poems Montale's reflections on his own personality and his present situation, add up to a realistically as well as metaphorically rich self-portrait, through which he analyzes what differentiates him from others, and what constitutes both his strength and his weakness. They blame me, he tells us in "Morgana," "for having abandoned/the herd almost as if I felt/I was illustrious, *ex gregis* or/goodness knows what." And in Montale, awareness of his own identity is inseparable from his insight into the nature and personality of the person loved. "They said"—

he comments on the kind of faith which he and his wife shared and which formed a most vital bond between them—

> . . . that we lacked faith.
> Perhaps we had a substitute for it.
> Faith is something else. They said
> but what's said isn't necessarily right.
> Perhaps faith in the Catastrophe would have been
> enough, but not for you
> who issued from the lap of the Gods
> to return there.

It is the essence of Montale's modernity that in spite of its dependence on pun and parody, satire and sarcasm, it is firmly rooted in the fundamental sobriety and integrity of his character. If, as he says in "In a Northern City," "One pays dearly for a modern soul," and that "I too might try one," he has not only tried, but tried supremely well to acquire "a modern soul," and what he has paid for so dearly is *our* gain as well as his, a lesson for us—both morally and poetically.

QUADERNO DI QUATTRO ANNI

IT DEPENDS: A POET'S NOTEBOOK

L'EDUCAZIONE INTELLETTUALE

Il grande tetto où picoraient des focs
è un'immagine idillica del mare.
Oggi la linea dell'orizzonte è scura
e la proda ribolle come una pentola.
Quando di qui passarono le grandi locomotive,
Bellerofonte, Orione i loro nomi,
tutte le forme erano liquescenti
per sovrappiù di giovinezza e il vento
più violento era ancora una carezza.

Un ragazzo col ciuffo si chiedeva
se l'uomo fosse un caso o un'intenzione,
se un lapsus o un trionfo . . . ma di chi?
Se il caso si presenta in un possibile
non è intenzione se non in un cervello.
E quale testa universale può
fare a meno di noi? C'era un dilemma
da decidere (non per gli innocenti).

Dicevano i Garanti che il vecchio logos
fosse tutt'uno coi muscoli dei fuochisti,
con le grandi zaffate del carbone,
con l'urlo dei motori, col tic tac
quasi dattilografico dell'Oltranza.
E il ragazzo col ciuffo non sapeva
se buttarsi nel mare a grandi bracciate
come se fosse vero che non ci si bagna
due volte nella stessa acqua.

2

INTELLECTUAL EDUCATION

The big roof *où picoraient des focs*
is an idyllic image of the sea.
Today the line of the horizon is dark
and the shore is boiling like a pot.
When the big locomotives
Bellerofonte, Orione, used to pass here
all the forms were liquescent
for excess of youth and the most
violent wind was still a caress.

A boy with a tuft of hair used to wonder
if man was a chance or an intention,
a mistake or a triumph . . . but whose?
If chance presents itself as a possibility
it isn't intention except in someone's brain.
And what universal head can do
without us? There was a dilemma
to be resolved (but not for the innocent).

The Guarantors used to say
that the old logos was all one with the muscles
of firemen, with the stench of coal,
with the screech of motors, and with the almost
typewriter-like tictac of the Extreme.
And the boy with the tuft didn't know
whether to throw himself into the sea
with outstretched arms as if it were true
that one can't bathe twice in the same water.

Il ragazzo col ciuffo non era poi
un infante se accanto a lui sorgevano
le Chimere, le larve di un premondo,
le voci dei veggenti e degli insani,
i volti dei sapienti, quelli ch'ebbero un nome
e che l'hanno perduto, i Santi e il princeps
dei folli, quello che ha baciato il muso
di un cavallo da stanga e fu da allora l'ospite
di un luminoso buio.
                              E passò molto tempo.
Tutto era poi mutato. Il mare stesso
s'era fatto peggiore. Ne vedo ora
crudeli assalti al molo, non s'infiocca
più di vele, non è il tetto di nulla,
neppure di se stesso.

LAGUNARE

Ancora un Erebo di più per farti
più rovente
e occultata per sempre nella mia vita,
da sempre un nodo che non può snodarsi.
Zattere e zolfo a lampi, inoccultabili questi,
alla deriva in un canale fumido,
non per noi agli imbarchi ma su un lubrico
insaccato di uomini e di gelo.
Non per me né per te se un punteruolo di diaspro
incide in noi lo stemma di chi resiste.

But then the boy with the tuft wasn't a baby
if there were conjured up beside him
the Chimeras, the ghosts of a preworld,
the voices of the seers and of the insane,
the faces of the wise, those who had a name
and who lost it, the saints and the prince
of the mad, he who kissed the nose
of a cart-horse and was ever after the guest
of a luminous darkness.

                        And much time passed.
Everything changed. The very sea got worse.
Now I see its cruel assaults on the pier,
it's no longer tasseled with sails,
it's the roof of nothing,
not even of itself.

FROM THE LAGOON

Still one more Erebus to make you
more fiery
and hidden for ever in my life,
for ever a knot that can't be unknotted.
Rafts and unconcealable
flashes of sulphur
adrift in a smoky canal;
not for us the landing stages
but a slippery crush of men and ice.
Not for me or for you if a jasper awl
engraves in us the coat of arms
of him who resists.

5

IL PIENO

Non serve un uragano di cavallette
a rendere insolcabile la faccia del mondo.
È vero ch'esse s'immillano, si immiliardano
e formano una scorza più compatta di un muro.
Ma il troppo pieno simula il troppo vuoto
ed è quello che basta a farci ammettere
questo scambio di barbe. Non fa male a nessuno.

DUE DESTINI

Celia fu resa scheletro dalle termiti
Clizia fu consumata dal suo Dio
ch'era lei stessa. Senza saperlo seppero
ciò che quasi nessuno dice vita.

INTERMEZZO

Il giardiniere
si ciba di funghi prataioli
eccellenti a suo dire,
sono scomparsi i ricci,
i dolcissimi irsuti maialini
delle forre,
la stagione è intermedia,
si va tra pozze d'acqua, il sole fa
trascolorare raggi sempre più rari,
a volte pare che corra, altre che sosti

FULLNESS

A swarm of locusts is no good
in making the face of the earth unplowable.
It's true they multiply into millions and billions
and form a crust more compact than a wall.
But what's too full simulates what's too empty
and it is that which makes us accept
any sudden change of roles.
It doesn't harm anyone.

TWO DESTINIES

Celia was reduced to a skeleton by termites
Clizia was consumed by her God
who was herself. Without knowing it they knew
what almost nobody calls life.

INTERMEZZO

The gardener
lives on field mushrooms which
he considers excellent, the hedgehogs
have disappeared, the sweet little bristly pigs
of the ravines, the season
is at the halfway stage,
one walks through puddles of water,
the sun makes its increasingly few rays
change color, at times it seems
to race, at others to rest lazily

impigrito o che scoppi addirittura;
anche il tempo del cuore è un'opinione,
la vita potrebbe coagularsi
e dire in un istante tutto quello
che meglio le occorreva per poi cedere
se stessa a un suo vicario.
È ciò che avviene a ogni volgere
di lunario e nessuno se ne avvede.

[NEI MIEI PRIMI ANNI]

Nei miei primi anni abitavo al terzo piano
e dal fondo del viale di pitòsfori
il cagnetto Galiffa mi vedeva
e a grandi salti dalla scala a chiocciola
mi raggiungeva. Ora non ricordo
se morì in casa nostra e se fu seppellito
e dove e quando. Nella memoria resta
solo quel balzo e quel guàito né
molto di più rimane dei grandi amori
quando non siano disperazione e morte.
Ma questo non fu il caso del bastardino
di lunghe orecchie che portava un nome
inventato dal figlio del fattore
mio coetaneo e analfabeta, vivo
meno del cane, è strano, nella mia insonnia.

or even to explode; the heart's
condition too is a matter of opinion,
life could coagulate
and say in an instant all
it most needed to say before
yielding itself to its substitute.
This is what happens every time
the calender changes and nobody notices it.

[IN MY EARLY YEARS]

In my early years I used to live
on the third floor and from the end of the
   pittosporum
avenue the little dog Galiffa
would see me and reach me with great bounds
up the winding stairs. Now I don't remember
if he died in our house, or if he was buried
and when and where. In memory
only that leap and that yelp remain,
nor does much more remain of great loves,
unless they signify desperation and death.
But this wasn't the case with the little mongrel,
with the long ears and a name invented for him
by the son of the bailiff who was
the same age as me, and illiterate,
and who is oddly enough
less alive than the dog in my insomnia.

[UN TEMPO]

Un tempo
tenevo sott'occhio l'atlante
degli uccelli scomparsi dalla faccia del mondo
opera di un allievo di David
ch'era fallito nel genere del quadro storico
o in altre monumentali prosopopee pittoriche.
Riflettevo su simili ipotetici atlanti
di vite senza becco e senza piume da millenni
irreperibili, insetti rettili pesci e anche
perché no? l'uomo stesso ma chi ne avrebbe
redatto o consultato l'opus magnum?
La scomparsa dell'uomo non farà una grinza
nel totale in faccende ben diverse
impelagato, orbo di chi abbia mezzi
di moto o riflessione, materia grigia e arti.
Forse la poesia sarà ancora salvata
da qualche raro fantasma peregrinante muto
e invisibile ignaro di se stesso. Ma è poi
l'arte della parola detta o scritta
accessibile a chi non ha voce e parola?
È tutta qui la mia povera idea
del linguaggio, questo dio demidiato
che non porta a salvezza perché non sa
nulla di noi e ovviamente
nulla di sé.

[ONCE]

Once
I used to peruse the atlas of birds
that have vanished from the face of the earth,
the work of a pupil of David who had
failed in the genre of historical painting
and other monumental artistic aspirations.
I was musing on hypothetical atlases
of lives without beaks, without feathers,
irretrievably lost through the millennia,
insects, reptiles, fish
and also, why not? man himself
but who would have compiled or consulted
his *opus magnum*?
The disappearance of man
fits in perfectly with the total
with its quite different involvements, and blind
as to who might have means of motion
or reflection; gray matter and crafts.
Perhaps poetry will still be saved
by some rare phantom wandering
mute, unseen, and unaware of itself.
But then is the art of the written or spoken word
accessible to one without voice or words?
This is all that my simple notion of language
amounts to, this god cut down to size
who doesn't lead one to salvation
for he knows nothing about us and obviously
nothing about himself.

A PIO RAJNA

Non amo i funerali. I pochi che ho seguito
anonimo in codazzi di dolenti
ma non mai troppo a lungo
mi sono usciti di memoria. Insiste
forse il più antico e quasi inesplicabile.
Quando un ometto non annunciato da ragli
di olifanti o da cozzi di durlindane
e non troppo dissimile dal Mime wagneriano
scese nell'ipogeo dove passavo ore e ore
e con balbuzie di ossequio e confusione mia
disse il suo nome io fui preso da un fulmine
e quel fuoco covò sotto la cenere
qualche tempo ma l'uomo non visse più a lungo.
Non era un artigiano di Valtellina
o un villico che offrisse rare bottiglie d'Inferno
ma tale che fece il nido negl'interstizi
delle più antiche saghe, quasi un uccello
senz'ali noto solo ai paleornitologi
o un esemplare di ciò che fu l'homo sapiens
prima che la sapienza fosse peccato.
C'è chi vive nel tempo che gli è toccato
ignorando che il tempo è reversibile
come un nastro di macchina da scrivere.
Chi scava nel passato può comprendere
che passato e futuro distano appena
di un milionesimo di attimo tra loro.
Per questo l'uomo era così piccolo,
per infiltrarsi meglio nelle fenditure.
Era un piccolo uomo o la memoria stenta

TO PIO RAJNA

I don't like funerals. The few I've attended
anonymously—but never for long—
among long queues of mourners have
gone out of my mind. If anything
the oldest one persists, almost inexplicably.
When a tiny man announced neither by the braying
of oliphants nor by the clashing of Durendals
and not too unlike a Wagnerian Mime
descended on the underground chamber where
I used to spend hours and hours,
and with obsequious stammerings and
to my utter confusion
told his name
I was struck by lightning and the fire
smoldered under the ashes for a while
but the man didn't live much longer.
He wasn't an artisan from Valtellina,
nor a peasant who would offer rare bottles
of Inferno, but one who made his nest among
the interstices of the oldest sagas,
almost a bird without wings known only
to the paleornithologists
or a model of what *Homo sapiens* was
before knowledge became sin.
There are some who live in the time
allotted to them, not knowing
that time is reversible like
the ribbon of a typewriter. He
who digs into the past would know

a ravvivarsi? Non so, ricordo solo
che non mancai quel funerale. Un giorno
come un altro, del '930.

[QUANDO COMINCIAI A DIPINGERE]

Quando cominciai a dipingere mia formica
tu eri incastrata nel gesso da cap-à-pie
la tavolozza era una crosta di vecchie tinte
fuse in un solo colore che lascio immaginare
diciamo di foglia secca io pensai altra cosa
e i risultati mostrarono che avevo visto giusto
ma come far nascere iridi da quella grumaglia stercale
di iridi neanche le tue sotto le lenti nere
come va? orrendamente dicesti ma certo c'è chi sta
   peggio.
Chissà se un inchiodato a un palo poteva parlare così
e forse così non avvenne tra i casi che si ricordano
un giorno in piazza Navona un luterano ventenne
saltò in una caldana di pece bollente
e fu per non ripudiare la sua fede (incredibile)
tu non toccasti quel grado di sublimità
non c'era una vasca bollente a portata di piede
né tu avresti potuto balzarvi con un salto

that barely a millionth of a second
divides the past from the future.
That's why the man was so small,
the better to fit into the crevices.
But was he a small man
or does my memory deceive me?
I don't know, the only thing I remember
is that I didn't miss that funeral.
It was a day like any other, in 1930.

[WHEN I BEGAN TO PAINT]

When I began to paint my ant
you were encased in plaster from head to foot
the palette was a crust of old colors fused
into a single hue which I leave
you to imagine let us say
of a dry leaf I thought of something else
and the outcome showed that I was right
but how to bring forth rainbows
from that dung-like encrustation of irises,
not even your own irises behind
the black lenses how are you?
rotten you said but no doubt there is somebody worse
    off.
Who knows if someone nailed to a pole
could speak like that and perhaps it didn't happen
among the cases one remembers one day
in Piazza Navona a twenty-year-old Lutheran
leaped into a cauldron of boiling pitch

senza essere neppure luterana, che imbroglio.
Fummo battuti in tutti i campi tu quasi viva
io con quei fogli degni di un immaginario
pittore Walter Closet.

SOTTO UN QUADRO LOMBARDO

Era il 12 ottobre del '982
mio natalizio
quando duecentomila laureati
disoccupati
in mancanza di meglio occuparono
palazzo Madama.
Sono disoccupato anch'io da sempre
obiettai a chi voleva malmenarmi.
Mi hanno buttato addosso un bianco accappatoio
e una cintura chermisina è vero
ma la mia vera occupazione il bandolo
del Vero
non l'ho trovata mai e ingiustamente muoio
sotto i vostri bastoni,
neppure voi lo troverete amici.
Indossate anche voi l'accappatoio
e saremo uno in più 200.000 e uno.
Dopodiché crollai su una poltrona
che fronteggiava un quadro del Cremona
e restava tranquillo lui solo nel tumulto.

rather than repudiate his (incredible) faith
you didn't attain that level of sublimity
there was no boiling pool within reach of your foot
nor could you have jumped into it with one leap
not even being a Lutheran, what a mess.
We were beaten in every field you almost alive
and I with these pages worthy of an imaginary
painter Walter Closet.

UNDER A LOMBARD PAINTING

12 October '982
was my birthday when
two hundred thousand
unemployed graduates
for want of something better to do
occupied Palazzo Madama.
I also have always been unemployed
I objected to those who wanted to maltreat me.
True they threw a white bathrobe around me
and a crimson belt
but I've never found my true occupation
the end of the skein of Truth
and I die unjustly under your blows,
neither would you find it my friends.
You too put on the bathrobe
and we shall be one more, 200,000 and one.
After which I sank into an armchair
facing a painting by Cremona
and he alone remained calm amid the tumult.

[SENZA MIA COLPA]

Senza mia colpa
mi hanno allogato in un hôtel meublé
dove non è servizio di ristorante.
Forse ne troverei uno non lontano
ma l'obliqua
furia dei carri mi spaventa. Resto
sprofondato in non molli piume, attento
a spirali di fumo dal portacenere.
Ma è quasi spento ormai il mozzicone.
Pure i suoni di fuori non si attenuano.
Ho pensato un momento ch'ero l'ultimo
dei viventi e che occulti celebranti
senza forma ma duri più di un muro
officiavano il rito per i defunti.
Inorridivo di essere il solo risparmiato
per qualche incaglio nel Calcolatore.
Ma non fu che un istante. Un'ombra bianca
mi sfiorò, un cameriere che serviva
l'aperitivo a un non so chi, ma vivo.

GLI UCCELLI PARLANTI

La morale dispone di poche parole
qualcuno ne ha contate quattrocento
e il record è finora imbattuto.

[THROUGH NO FAULT OF MINE]

Through no fault of mine
they have put me up in a *hôtel meublé*
with no restaurant service.
Perhaps I should find one not far away
but the driving fury of the vans
frightens me. I remain sunk
in feathers far from soft,
and watch the spirals of smoke
from the ashtray. But the butt is now
almost extinguished. And yet
the sounds from outside don't subside.
I thought for a moment that I was
the last of the living and that
occult celebrants without form
but harder than a wall
officiated at the rites of the dead.
I was shocked to be the only one saved
as a result of some hitch in the Calculator.
But it was only for a second.
A white shadow brushed past me,
a waiter serving an aperitif to someone
I don't know who, but alive.

THE TALKING BIRDS

Morals have few words at their disposal.
Someone counted four hundred
and the record is still unbeaten.

Neppure gli uccelli indiani
che oggi sono di moda
e somigliano a merli
rapace becco di fuoco e penne neroblù
riescono a dirne di più.
La differenza è nelle risate:
quella del falso merlo non è la nostra,
ha un suo bersaglio, l'uomo che si crede
più libero di lui: di me che passo
ogni giorno e saluto quel gomitolo
di piume e suoni destinato a vivere
meno di me. Così si dice, ma . . .

A RITROSO

Fra i miei ascendenti qualcuno
lottò per l'Unità d'Italia
raggiunse alti gradi, portò
la greca sul berretto, fu coinvolto
in brogli elettorali. Non gl'importava
forse nulla di nulla, non m'importa
nulla di lui; il suo sepolcro rischia
di essere scoperchiato per carenza
di terra o marmi o altro. C'è una morte
cronologica, una che è economica
un'altra che non c'è perché non se ne parla.
Quanti antenati occorrono a chi un giorno
scriverà quattro versi zoppicanti
quanti togati lestofanti o asini

Not even the Indian birds which are
the fashion nowadays and which
resemble blackbirds with their fiery
predatory beaks and blue-black feathers
can manage to say more.
The difference lies in their laughter:
the false blackbird's isn't like ours,
it has its target, man
who thinks he is more free than the blackbird:
or than I who pass each day
and salute that ball of feathers and sounds
destined to live less than me.
Or so they say, but . . .

GOING BACKWARDS

Among my ancestors someone
fought for the unification of Italy;
reached a high rank, wore zigzag braid
on his cap, was embroiled in electoral
intrigues. Perhaps nothing mattered to him
and nothing of him matters to me;
his tomb is in danger of being uncovered
for lack of earth, marble or something.
There's a chronological death, an economic one,
and another that isn't there because
nobody talks about it.
How many ancestors does he need
who will one day write
four limping verses, how many

di sette cotte. E di lì può nascere
persino la cultura o la Kultur!

IL SABIÀ

Il sabià canta a terra, non sugli alberi
così disse una volta un poeta senz'ali,
e anticipò la fine di ogni vegetale.
Esiste poi chi non canta né sopra né sotto
e ignoro se è uccello o uomo o altro animale.
Esiste, forse esisteva, oggi è ridotto
a nulla o quasi. È già troppo per quel che vale.

IL GIORNO DEI MORTI

La Gina ha acceso un candelotto per i suoi morti.
L'ha acceso in cucina, i morti sono tanti e non vicini.
Bisogna risalire a quando era bambina
e il caffelatte era un pugno di castagne secche.
Bisogna ricreare un padre piccolo e vecchio
e alle sue scarpinate per trovarle un poco di vino
    dolce.
Di vini lui non poteva berne né dolci né secchi
perché mancavano i soldi e c'era da nutrire
i porcellini che lei portava al pascolo.
Tra i morti si può mettere la maestra che dava
    bacchettate

togaed cheats or perfectly
asinine asses. And from this
there might emerge even culture or kultur!

THE SABIÀ

The sabià sings on the ground, not in the trees,
so said a poet without wings
once, and he predicted the end of all vegetable life.
Then there's someone
who sings neither above nor below
and I don't know if he's a bird, a man or an animal.
He exists, or existed perhaps; today
he's reduced to nothing or almost.
And it's already too much for what it's worth.

ALL SOULS' DAY

Gina has lit a candle for her dead.
She has lit it in the kitchen, the dead
are many and not close to her.
One has to go back in time to her childhood
when a handful of dry chestnuts was
milk and coffee. One has to re-create
a little old father and his long slow walks
in search of a drop of sweet wine for her.
He himself couldn't drink either sweet or dry wine
for there was no money and there were the piglets to
    be fed
which she used to bring to pasture.

alle dita gelate della bambina. Morto
anche qualche vivente, semivivente prossimo
al traghetto. È una folla che non è niente
perché non ha portato al pascolo i porcellini.

[LA VITA L'INFINITA BOLLA]

La vita l'infinita
bolla dell'esistibile ha deciso
di spogliarsi dei suoi contenuti.
Non erano necessari se poté farne a meno
pure vi fu un istante in cui lei disse un poco
di guardaroba può tornarmi comodo.
Furono pelli di caproni e smoking a tre pezzi
la giacca bianca per festival estivi
bionde parrucche d'asino per femmine pelate
e ragnatele a non finire il balsamo
che cura ogni ferita.
Poi la proliferazione salì al cielo
lo raggiunse ed infine parve stanca.
Che più ti resta disse il poeta Monti
e in effetti restava poco o nulla
e non quello che conta. Stolto il Vate
come tutti i suoi pari non s'avvide
che se è vero che il più contiene il meno
il più potrebbe anche stancarsi, non ne mancano
le avvisaglie.

Among the dead one can include the schoolmistress
who caned the child's frozen hands.
Among the living too some are dead,
some half-alive and on the point of boarding
the ferry. A crowd which is nothing because
it hasn't brought the piglets to pasture.

[LIFE THE INFINITE BUBBLE]

Life the infinite bubble
of the existible has decided
to strip itself of its contents.
They weren't necessary if it could do without them
and yet there was an instant when it said
a few wardrobe items might come in handy.
Goatskin coats three-piece dinner suits a white
jacket for summer festivals blond
donkey-hair wigs for bald women
and endless cobwebs the balm
which heals every wound.
Then the proliferation rose to heaven
reached it and in the end seemed tired.
What more remains for you asked the poet
Monti and in fact very little remained
or nothing or at any rate nothing that counts.
The foolish poet like all his kind
didn't realize that if it is true
that the more contains the less the more
could also get tired, signs of it
are not lacking.

RIFLESSI NELL'ACQUA

Il consumo non può per necessità
obliterare la nostra pelle.
Sopprimendo la quale . . . ma qui il monologante
si specchiò nel ruscello. Vi si vedeva
una sua emanazione ma disarticolata
e sbilenca che poi sparve addirittura.
Un nulla se n'è andato ch'era anche parte
di me, disse: la fine può procedere
a passo di lumaca. E pensò ad altro.

L'ONORE
a Guido Piovene

Un giorno mi dicevi
che avresti ritenuto grande onore
lucidare le scarpe
di Cecco Beppe il vecchio Imperatore.
Si era presso il confine ma non oltre
la terra delle chiacchiere in cui sei nato.
Mi dichiarai d'accordo anche se un giorno
senza sparare un colpo
della mia Webley Scott 7,65
senza uccidere senza possedere
neanche un'ombra dell'arte militare
avevo fatto fronte ai pochi stracci
dell'oste avversa. Ma mi chiesi pure
quale fosse la briciola d'onore
che mi era scivolata tra le dita
e non me n'ero accorto. C'è sempre un paio di stivali

REFLECTIONS IN THE WATER

Wear and tear cannot of necessity
obliterate our skin.
Suppressing which . . . but here the monologist
saw his reflection in the stream.
He saw his emanation there, disjointed
and distorted and eventually it disappeared.
A mere nothing is gone which was also
part of me, he said: the end can move
at a snail's pace. And he thought of something else.

HONOR
To Guido Piovene

One day you told me that
you would have considered it a great honor
to polish the shoes
of the old Emperor Franz Joseph. It was
near the border but not beyond
the land of gossip where you were born.
I agreed, even though one day,
without firing a shot
from my Webley Scott 7.65
without killing without knowing
a thing about the military art,
I had faced the tattered remnants
of the hostile army. But still
I wondered what the crumb of honor was
which had slipped through my fingers
without my noticing it. There is

che attendono la spazzola il lustrino,
c'è sempre il punto anche se impercettibile
per il quale si può senza sprecarla
usare una parola come onore.
Non è questione di stivali o altri
imbiancamenti di sepolcri. Il fatto è
che l'onore ci appare quando è impossibile,
quando somiglia come due gocce d'acqua
al suo gemello, la vergogna. Un lampo
tra due confini non territoriali,
una luce che abbuia tutto il resto
questo è l'onore che non abbiamo avuto
perché la luce non è fatta solo
per gli occhi. È questo il mio ricordo, il solo
che nasce su un confine e non lo supera.

LA MEMORIA

La memoria fu un genere letterario
da quando non era nata la scrittura.
Divenne poi cronaca e tradizione
ma già puzzava di cadavere.
La memoria vivente è immemoriale,
non sorge dalla mente, non vi si sprofonda.
Si aggiunge all'esistente come un'aureola
di nebbia al capo. È già sfumata, è dubbio
che ritorni. Non ha sempre memoria
di sé.

always a pair of boots waiting for the brush
and the polish, there is always the point
even if imperceptible for which one can use
a word like honor without wasting it.
It's not a question of boots or other forms
of whitewashing the sepulcher. The fact is
that honor appears to us when it's impossible,
when like two drops of water
it resembles its twin, shame.
A flash of lightning between two non-territorial
boundaries, a light that darkens
all the rest this is the honor we haven't had
because light isn't made only for the eyes.
This is what I remember, the only thing
which is born on a border and doesn't cross it.

MEMORY

Memory was a literary genre
before writing was born.
Then it became chronicle and tradition
but it was already stinking like a corpse.
Living memory is immemorial,
it doesn't arise from the mind,
nor sink into it. It clings
to whatever exists like a halo
of fog around the head.
It has already evaporated and it's doubtful
if it will return. It doesn't
always remember itself.

BIG BANG O ALTRO

Mi pare strano che l'universo
sia nato da un'esplosione,
mi pare strano che si tratti invece
del formicolìo di una stagnazione.

Ancora più incredibile che sia uscito
dalla bacchetta magica
di un dio che abbia caratteri
spaventosamente antropomorfici.

Ma come si può pensare che tale macchinazione
sia posta a carico di chi sarà vivente,
ladro e assassino fin che si vuole ma
sempre innocente?

LA SOLITUDINE

Se mi allontano due giorni
i piccioni che beccano
sul davanzale
entrano in agitazione
secondo i loro obblighi corporativi.
Al mio ritorno l'ordine si rifà
con supplemento di briciole
e disappunto del merlo che fa la spola
tra il venerato dirimpettaio e me.
A così poco è ridotta la mia famiglia.
E c'è chi n'ha una o due, che spreco ahimè!

BIG BANG OR SOMETHING ELSE

It seems strange to me that the universe
should have resulted from an explosion,
likewise strange that it should instead
be due to the swarming of a stagnation.

It is even more incredible that
it should have issued from the magic rod
of a god with frighteningly
anthropomorphic features.

But how can one lay such a machination at the
    door
of him who will be living,
thief or assassin, as much as you like,
but always innocent?

SOLITUDE

If I go away for a couple of days
the pigeons that peck
on my windowsill start agitating
according to the directives of their union.
When I return order is restored
with a supplement of crumbs and of disappointment
for the blackbird that goes to and fro
between the venerable old man opposite me
and myself. My family is reduced
to so little. And some have one
or more, alas what a waste!

IL VUOTO

È sparito anche il vuoto
dove un tempo si poteva rifugiarsi.
Ora sappiamo che anche l'aria
è una materia che grava su di noi.
Una materia immateriale, il peggio
che poteva toccarci.
Non è pieno abbastanza perché dobbiamo
popolarlo di fatti, di movimenti
per poter dire che gli apparteniamo
e mai gli sfuggiremo anche se morti.
Inzeppare di oggetti quello ch'è
il solo Oggetto per definizione
senza che a lui ne importi niente o turpe
commedia. E con che zelo la recitiamo!

DOPOPIOGGIA

Sulla rena bagnata appaiono ideogrammi
a zampa di gallina. Guardo addietro
ma non vedo rifugi o asili di volatili.
Sarà passata un'anatra stanca, forse azzoppata.
Non saprei decrittare quel linguaggio
se anche fossi cinese. Basterà un soffio
di vento a scancellarlo. Non è vero
che la Natura sia muta. Parla a vanvera
e la sola speranza è che non si occupi
troppo di noi.

THE VOID

Even the void has disappeared
where one could once take refuge.
Now we know that even the air
is matter that weighs upon us.
Immaterial matter, the worst
that could have befallen us.
It isn't full enough because
we must people it with facts and actions
to be able to say we belong to it
and will never escape it even when dead.
To cram with objects what is
the sole Object by definition although
it doesn't care for it oh what a vile
comedy. And with what zeal we perform it!

AFTER THE RAIN

On the wet sand ideograms appear
like a hen's claws. I look back but see
neither bird sanctuaries nor shelters.
A tired or perhaps a lame duck
may have passed. I wouldn't be able to decipher
that language even if I were Chinese.
One gust of wind will be enough to cancel it.
It isn't true that Nature is mute.
It speaks at random and the only hope is
it doesn't bother too much about us.

L'EROISMO

Clizia mi suggeriva di ingaggiarmi
tra i guerriglieri di Spagna e più di una volta mi
    sento
morto a Guadalajara o superstite illustre
che mal reggesi in piedi dopo anni di galera.
Ma nulla di ciò avvenne: nemmeno il torrentizio
verbo del comiziante redimito di gloria
e d'alti incarchi mi regalò la sorte.
Ma dove ho combattuto io che non amo
il gregge degli inani e dei fuggiaschi?
Qualche cosa ricordo. Un prigioniero *mio*
che aveva in tasca un Rilke e fummo amici
per pochi isanti; e inutili fatiche
e tonfi di bombarde e il fastidioso
ticchettìo dei cecchini.
Ben poco e anche inutile per lei
che non amava le patrie e n'ebbe una per caso.

LEGGENDO CAVAFIS

Mentre Nerone dorme placido nella sua
traboccante bellezza
i suoi piccoli lari che hanno udito
le voci delle Erinni lasciano il focolare
in grande confusione. Come e quando

HEROISM

Clizia used to suggest
that I should join the guerrilla fighters of Spain
and more than once I feel I have died
at Guadalajara or that I'm an illustrious survivor
who can barely stand on his feet
after years of imprisonment. But
nothing of all this happened: fate didn't
even endow me with the gift of torrential
speech like one crowned with glory
and high offices, addressing a political rally.
But where did I fight—I who don't love
the herd of the inane and the fugitives?
I remember something. One of *my* prisoners
had a book of Rilke in his pocket
and we were friends for a few seconds;
vain labors the thud of bombardments
and the vexatious tictac of the sharpshooters.
Not much and even at that quite useless
for her who didn't love mother countries
and had one by chance.

READING CAVAFY

While Nero sleeps placidly in
his overflowing beauty
his little household gods who have heard
the voices of the Furies leave
the hearth in great confusion.

si desterà? Così disse il Poeta.
Io, sovrano di nulla, neppure di me stesso
senza il tepore di odorosi legni
e lambito dal gelo di un aggeggio
a gasolio,
io pure ascolto suoni tictaccanti
di zoccoli e di piedi, ma microscopici.
Non mi sveglio, ero desto già da un pezzo
e non mi attendo ulteriori orrori
oltre i già conosciuti.
Neppure posso imporre a qualche famulo
di tagliarmi le vene. Nulla mi turba. Ho udito
lo zampettìo di un topolino. Trappole
non ne ho mai possedute.

TESTIMONI DI GEOVA

Quasi ogni giorno mi scrive
un testimone di Geova
che mi prepari all'Evento.
Il male è che questo totale
capovolgimento
non offre confortevoli prospettive.
Se finisce chi vive
e vivo non fu mai
e risorge nel modo più gradevole
a me perché invisibile
temo che i suoi segnali mi pervengano
magari in cifra

When and how will he wake up?
So said the Poet. I, the sovereign of nothing,
not even of myself, without the warmth
of the odorous wood and lapped
by the frost of an oil-fired device,
I too hear the microscopic tictac
of hooves and feet.
I don't wake up, I've already been awake
for quite some time and don't expect other horrors
than those already known.
I can't even order a manservant
to cut my veins for me.
Nothing upsets me. I have heard the pattering of a
      mouse.
And I have never possessed mousetraps.

JEHOVAH'S WITNESSES

Almost every day
a Jehovah's Witness writes to me
that I should prepare for the Event.
The trouble is
that this total upheaval
holds out no comfortable prospects.
If he who lives dies
—and he was never alive—
and rises again in a way
most gratifying to me
because invisible, I fear
its signals might reach me

per ammonirmi che il congedo vero
è sempre in prova.
Se fu triste il pensiero della morte
quello che il Tutto dura
è il più pauroso.

L'ARMONIA

L'armonia è un quid raro
Adelheit
non è oggetto né fluido né sostanza
e non sempre ha il lucore della gemma.
L'armonia è di chi è entrato nella vena giusta
del cristallo e non sa né vuole uscirne.
L'armonia è vera quando non tocca il fondo,
non è voluta da chi non la conosce
non è creduta da chi ne ha il sospetto.
A volte l'ippocastano
lascia cadere un suo duro frutto
sulla calvizie di chi non saprà mai
se fu eletto o scacciato per abiezione.
L'armonia è dei segnati ma il patto è
che ne siano inconsapevoli. E tu
Adelheit lo sai da tanto tempo.
Hai conosciuto il tuo segreto senza
che il dio che la elargisce se ne accorga
e sarai sempre salva. Anche gli dèi
possono addormentarsi (ma con occhio solo).

perhaps in ciphers
to warn me that the true leave-taking
is always being tried out.
If the thought of death was sad,
the thought that All will last
is the most frightening.

HARMONY

Harmony is something rare
Adelheit,
it's neither object, nor fluid nor substance
and it doesn't always have the glitter
of a gem. Harmony belongs
to him who has entered the right vein
of the crystal and neither wants to nor can get out.
Harmony is real when it doesn't touch the bottom,
it isn't willed by him who doesn't know it,
nor believed by him who suspects it.
At times the horse-chestnut
drops its hard fruit on the baldness
of him who will never know if
he was elected or rejected for abjectness.
Harmony belongs to the chosen
but on condition that they're unaware of it.
You Adelheit have long known it.
You have known your secret without
the god who bestows it noticing it
and you will always be safe. Even the gods
can fall asleep (but with one eye open).

I TRAVESTIMENTI

Non è poi una favola
che il diavolo si presenti
come già il grande Fregoli
travestito.
Ma il vero *travesti*
che fu uno dei cardini
del vecchio melodramma
non è affatto esaurito.
Non ha per nulla bisogno
di trucchi parrucche o altro.
Basta un'occhiata allo specchio
per credersi altri.
Altri e sempre diversi
ma sempre riconoscibili
da chi s'è fatto un cliché
del nostro volto.
Risulta così sempre vana
l'arte dello sdoppiamento:
abbiamo voluto camuffarci
come i prostituti nottivaghi
per nascondere meglio le nostre piaghe
ma è inutile, basta guardarci.

L'OPINIONE

Al tempo dei miei primi vaneggiamenti
non era ancora nata l'Opinione.
Ora essa dilaga, s'è persino cacciata

DISGUISES

It is not after all a fairy tale
that the devil appears in drag
like the great Fregoli.
But the true *travesti*
who was one of the pivots
of old melodramas
is by no means exhausted.
He doesn't need makeup at all,
wigs or anything else.
A glance in the mirror is enough
to make us believe we are somebody else.
Somebody else and always different
but always recognizable by him
who has made a cliché of our faces.
Thus the art of the split personality
always turns out to be useless.
We wanted to camouflage ourselves
like the transvestites wandering by night
the better to hide our wounds,
but in vain,
it's enough to look at us.

OPINION

At the time of my first ravings
Opinion wasn't yet born.
Now it is rife, it has even gotten

nelle scuole elementari.
Sempre meno opinabile l'incontro con un Messia
inascoltato che dica non pensate.
La vita non ha molto da fare
con l'uomo e tanto meno con le idee.
E che avrebbe da fare poi la vita?
Questo non è insegnato dalle mirabili
sorti di cui si ciarla.
C'è chi lo sa magari ma ha la bocca
sigillata e non parla.

UN POETA

Poco filo mi resta, ma spero che avrò modo
di dedicare al prossimo tiranno
i miei poveri carmi. Non mi dirà di svenarmi
come Nerone a Lucano. Vorrà una lode spontanea
scaturita da un cuore riconoscente
e ne avrà ad abbondanza. Potrò egualmente
lasciare orma durevole. In poesia
quello che conta non è il contenuto
ma la Forma.

PER UN FIORE RECISO

Spenta in tenera età
può dirsi che hai reso diverso il mondo?

into the primary schools. The encounter
with a Messiah that nobody listens to
and who might ask us not to think,
is becoming increasingly improbable.
Life hasn't got much to do
with man, and still less with ideas.
Then what would the role of life be?
This is not taught by the wonderful destinies
one chatters about. Maybe there's someone
who knows it but his mouth is sealed.

A POET

Only a short thread is left me
but I hope I'll be able to dedicate
my humble songs to the next tyrant.
He won't ask me to cut my veins
as Nero asked Lucan. He will want
spontaneous praise gushing from a grateful
heart and will have it in abundance.
All the same I shall be able to leave
a lasting trace. In poetry
what matters is not the content
but the form.

FOR A CUT FLOWER

Can one say that having been nipped
in the bud you made the world different?

Questa è per me certezza che non posso
comunicare ad altri. Non si è mai certi
di noi stessi che pure abbiamo occhi
e mani per vederci, per toccarci.
Una traccia invisibile non è per questo
meno segnata? Te lo dissi un giorno
e tu: è un fatto che non mi riguarda.
Sono la capinera che dà un trillo
e a volte lo ripete ma non si sa
se è quella o un'altra. E non potresti farlo
neanche te che hai orecchio.

SOTTO LA PERGOLA

Sulla pergola povera di foglie
vanno e vengono i topi in perfetto equilibrio.
Non uno che cadesse nella nostra zuppiera.
Credo ne siano passate
negli anni più generazioni
in una quasi simbiosi
con gli occupanti di sotto.
Certo non era poca la differenza
di status, di abitudini e di lingua.
Di lingua soprattutto. Nullameno
l'intesa era perfetta e nessun gatto
sperimentò l'ascesa della pergola.
Mi resta qualche dubbio sulla zuppiera
che suggerisce immagini patriarcali
del tutto aliene dalla mia memoria.

This is a certainty for me
which I can't communicate to others.
We are never sure of ourselves even though
we have eyes and hands with which
to see ourselves, touch ourselves.
Is a groove carved less deeply for being
invisible? I told you so
one day and you: it doesn't concern me.
I'm the blackcap which makes a trilling sound
and repeats it at times but one doesn't know
if it's this blackcap or another. And even you
who have ears wouldn't be able to tell.

UNDER THE BOWER

Under the thinly leafed bower the mice
come and go in perfect balance.
Not one fell into our soup tureen.
I think many generations of mice
have passed through the years in a quasi
symbiosis with the occupants below.
To be sure the difference in status,
customs and language wasn't negligible.
Above all in language. Nonetheless
the accord was perfect and no cat
ever tried to climb the bower.
But I have some doubts as to the soup tureen,
which suggests patriarchal images
quite foreign to my memory.
There never was any soup tureen, never

Non ci fu mai zuppiera, mai dinastie
di roditori sul mio capo, mai
nulla che ora sia vivo nella mia mente.
Fu tuttavia perfetta con ore di tripudio
la reticenza, quella che sta ai margini
e non s'attuffa perché il mare è ancora
un vuoto, un supervuoto e già ne abbiamo
fin troppo, un vuoto duro come un sasso.

STORIA DI TUTTI I GIORNI

L'unica scienza che resti in piedi
l'escatologia
non è una scienza, è un fatto
di tutti i giorni.
Si tratta delle briciole che se ne vanno
senza essere sostituite.
Che importano le briciole va borbottando
l'aruspice,
è la torta che resta, anche sbrecciata
se qua e là un po' sgonfiata.
Tutto sta in una buona stagionatura,
cent'anni più di dieci, mille anni più di cento
ne accresceranno il sapore.
Ovviamente sarà più fortunato
l'assaggiatore futuro senza saperlo
e « il resto è letteratura ».

any dynasties of rodents over my head,
never anything which may now be alive
in my mind. And yet in hours
of jubilation the reticence was perfect,
that which remains on the banks
and never dives because the sea is still
a void, a supervoid and we
already have too much of it,
a void hard as a rock.

EVERYDAY HISTORY

Eschatology,
the only science which holds water,
is not a science, it's a fact
of everyday life.
It is a question of crumbs that vanish
without being replaced.
What do the crumbs matter, grumbles
the haruspex,
it is the cake that remains, even if cracked
and somewhat flattened here and there.
Everything depends on a good seasoning,
a hundred years more than ten,
a thousand more than a hundred
will improve its flavor.
Obviously the future taster will be
luckier without knowing it and
"the rest is literature."

ELOGIO DEL NOSTRO TEMPO

Non si può esagerare abbastanza
l'importanza del mondo
(del nostro, intendo)
probabilmente il solo
in cui si possa uccidere
con arte e anche creare
opere d'arte destinate a vivere
lo spazio di un mattino, sia pur fatto
di millenni e anche più. No, non si può
magnificarlo a sufficienza. Solo
ci si deve affrettare perché potrebbe
non essere lontana
l'ora in cui troppo si sarà gonfiata
secondo un noto apologo la rana.

IL FUOCO E IL BUIO

Qualche volta la polvere da sparo
non prende fuoco per umidità,
altre volte s'accende senza il fiammifero
o l'acciarino.
Basterebbe il tascabile briquet
se ci fosse una goccia di benzina.
E infine non occorre fuoco affatto,
anzi un buon sottozero tiene a freno
la tediosa bisava, l'Ispirazione.
Non era troppo arzilla giorni fa
ma incerottava bene le sue rughe.

EULOGY OF OUR TIMES

One cannot exaggerate enough
the importance of the world
(our own, I mean)
probably the only one
in which one can kill with art
and even create
works of art destined to live
for the space of a morning, although made
of millennia or even more.
No, one can't magnify it enough.
Just that we had better get a move on
for the hour may not be far-off
when according to a well-known fable
the frog will be too swollen.

THE FIRE AND THE DARKNESS

Sometimes gunpowder doesn't ignite
because of the damp, at others
it ignites without a match or the flintlock.
A cigarette lighter would do
if there were some fluid in it.
In the end one doesn't need fire at all.
In fact a few degrees below zero
keeps in check
that tedious great-grandmother Inspiration.
She wasn't very sprightly some days back
but she bandaged her wrinkles well.

Ora pare nascosta tra le pieghe
della tenda e ha vergogna di se stessa.
Troppe volte ha mentito, ora può scendere
sulla pagina il buio il vuoto il niente.
Di questo puoi fidarti amico scriba.
Puoi credere nel buio quando la luce mente.

LE STORIE LETTERARIE

Sono sempre d'avviso
che Shakespeare fosse una cooperativa.
Che per le buffonate si serviva
di cerretani pari a lui nel genio
ma incuranti di tutto fuorché dei soldi.
Non può ingoiare troppo la sopravvivenza.
A volte digerisce un plotone, tale altra
distilla poche sillabe e butta un monumento
nel secchio dei rifiuti. Produce come i funghi,
puoi trovarne parecchi tutt'insieme, poi resti
a mani vuote per un giorno intero
o per un anno o un secolo. Dipende.

SOLILOQUIO

Il canale scorre silenzioso
maleodorante
questo è il palazzo dove fu composto
il Tristano

Now she seems to be hidden among
the folds of the curtain and
is ashamed of herself. She has lied
too often, now darkness, void, nothingness
can all descend on the page.
You can be sure of this, fellow-scribbler.
You can trust the darkness when the light lies.

LITERARY HISTORIES

I have always been of the opinion
that Shakespeare was a cooperative.
That for his jests he always used charlatans
like himself in genius but careless
of everything else except money.
Survival can't swallow too much.
At times it digests a platoon,
at others it distills a few syllables
and throws a monument into the wastebasket.
It reproduces like mushrooms, you might find
a whole lot of them at once, and then
you are empty-handed for a whole day,
or a year or a century. It depends.

SOLILOQUY

The canal flows silently
malodorously
this is the palace where Tristan
was composed and there

ed ecco il buco dove Henry James
gustò le crêpes suzette —
non esistono più i grandi uomini
ne restano inattendibili biografie
nessuno certo scriverà la mia —
gli uomini di San Giorgio sono più importanti
di tanti altri e di me ma non basta non basta —
il futuro ha appetito non si contenta più
di hors-d'oeuvre e domanda schidionate
di volatili frolli, nauseabonde delizie —
il futuro è altresì disappetente
può volere una crosta ma che crosta
quale non fu mai vista nei menus —
il futuro è anche onnivoro e non guarda
per il sottile — Qui è la casa dove
visse più anni un pederasta illustre
assassinato altrove — Il futuro è per lui —
non è nulla di simile nella mia vita
nulla che sazi le bramose fauci
del futuro

SERA DI PASQUA

Alla televisione
Cristo in croce cantava come un tenore

the hole where Henry James
tasted *crêpes suzette*—
but great men don't exist anymore
what remains of them
is their unreliable biographies
certainly no one will write mine—
the men of San Giorgio are more important
than so many others and me
but it's not enough not enough—the future
is hungry it no longer contents
itself with *hors-d'oeuvre* but
demands spits crammed with tender birds,
nauseating delights—the future
is likewise unappetizing
it might want a crust but what a crust!
such as was never seen in the menus—
the future is also omnivorous
and doesn't look for subtleties—
Here is the house where for years
lived a famous pederast who was murdered
    elsewhere—
The future belongs to him—
there is nothing like that in my life
nothing to satiate the ravenous
jaws of the future

EASTER SUNDAY EVENING

On the television
Christ on the cross was singing

53

colto da un'improvvisa
colica *pop*.
Era stato tentato poco prima
dal diavolo vestito da donna nuda.
Questa è la religione del ventesimo secolo.
Probabilmente la notte di San Bartolomeo
o la coda troncata di una lucertola
hanno lo stesso peso nell'Economia
dello Spirito
fondata sul principio dell'Indifferenza.
Ma forse bisogna dire che non è vero
bisogna dire che è vera la falsità,
poi si vedrà che cosa accade. Intanto
chiudiamo il video. Al resto
provvederà chi può (se questo *chi*
ha qualche senso). Noi non lo sapremo.

PASQUETTA

La mia strada è privilegiata
vi sono interdette le automobili
e presto anche i pedoni (a mia eccezione
e di pochi scortati da gorilla).
O beata solitudo disse il Vate.
Non ce n'è molta nelle altre strade.
L'intellighenzia a cui per mia sciagura
appartenevo si è divisa in due.
C'è chi si immerge e c'è chi non s'immerge.
C'est emmerdant si dice da una parte

like a tenor overcome by
a sudden attack of pop colic.
A short while before he had been tempted
by the devil in the guise of a naked woman.
This is twentieth-century religion.
Probably St. Bartholomew's night
or the truncated tail of a lizard
have the same weight
in the Economy of the Spirit
founded on the principle of Indifference.
But perhaps one should say that it isn't true,
one should say that the false is true
and then we shall see what happens.
In the meantime let's turn off the T.V. set.
He who can will look after the rest
(if this *he* means anything) we
wouldn't know.

EASTER MONDAY

My street is a privileged one where
cars are forbidden and soon
pedestrians too will be
(except myself and a few others
escorted by bodyguards). O blessed solitude,
said the Poet. There isn't much of it in
other streets. The intelligentsia to which
I had the misfortune of belonging
is divided into two. There are those
who immerse themselves and those who don't.

e dall'altra. Chi sa da quale parte
ci si immerda di meno. La questione
non è d'oggi soltanto. Il saggio sperimenta
le due alternative in una volta sola.
Io sono troppo vecchio per sostare
davanti al bivio. C'era forse un trivio
e mi ha scelto. Ora è tardi per recedere.

[SUB TEGMINE FAGI]

Sub tegmine fagi
non si starà molto allegri
sotto alberi di stucco.

Se non fosse così
perché/su chi si abbatterebbe il grande
colpo di scopa?

[HO SPARSO DI BECCHIME]

Ho sparso di becchime il davanzale
per il concerto di domani all'alba.
Ho spento il lume e ho atteso il sonno.
E sulla passerella già comincia
la sfilata dei morti grandi e piccoli
che ho conosciuto in vita. Arduo distinguere
tra chi vorrei o non vorrei che fosse
ritornato tra noi. Là dove stanno

C'est emmerdant says this group and that.
Who knows which side stinks less.
The question doesn't concern only the present.
The wise man tries both alternatives at once.
I'm too old to wait at the crossroads.
Perhaps there was a junction of three
roads and it chose me. Now
it's too late to back out.

[SUB TEGMINE FAGI]

Sub tegmine fagi
one won't be very cheerful
under stucco trees.

If it were not so
why/on whom would the great
stroke of the broom fall?

[I HAVE SCATTERED BIRDSEED]

I have scattered birdseed on the sill
for tomorrow's dawn concert. I have
turned off the light and waited for sleep.
Already on the gangway begins
the procession of the dead both great
and small I knew in life.
It's difficult to distinguish between
those I would and those I wouldn't like

sembrano inalterabili per un di più
di sublimata corruzione. Abbiamo
fatto del nostro meglio per peggiorare il mondo.

[RUIT HORA]

RUIT HORA che tragico pasticcio.
È troppo lenta l'ora per essere un baleno,
quel brevissimo istante che farebbe ridicolo
tutto il resto.
Ma l'ora è come un fulmine per chi vorrebbe
restare sulla terra a piedi fermi
e non già su una palla rotolante
in uno spazio che non avendo fine
non può nemmeno avere un senso. Questo
lo ha soltanto un finito, uno che non finisce
e sia desiderabile, perfetto.
                                        È un grattacapo
di più, inevitabile — e anche orrendo.

[MEZZO SECOLO FA]

Mezzo secolo fa
sono apparsi i cuttlefishbones
mi dice uno straniero addottorato
che intende gratularmi.
Vorrei mandarlo al diavolo. Non amo
essere conficcato nella storia
per quattro versi o poco più. Non amo
chi sono, ciò che sembro. È stato tutto
un qui pro quo. E ora chi n'esce fuori?

to return among us. They seem
unalterable where they stand
because of a more sublimated corruption.
We've done our best to make the world worse.

[RUIT HORA]

RUIT HORA what a tragic mess.
The hour's too sluggish to be a flash,
that briefest instant which would make all the rest
ridiculous. But the hour is like lightning
to him who would like to stand firmly
on the earth and not on a rolling ball
in a space which not having an end
has no meaning either. Only he
who is finite can have a meaning, he
who doesn't finish and may be
desirable, perfect.
                    An additional bother,
inevitable—and also horrible.

[HALF A CENTURY AGO]

Half a century ago
the cuttlefishbones appeared
a learned foreigner tells me
by way of congratulating me.
I would like to tell him to go to the devil.
I don't like being nailed down to history
for four verses or little more.
I don't like who I am who I seem
to be. It has all been a *quid pro quo*.
And who can get out of that now?

[LA CAPINERA]

La capinera non fu uccisa
da un cacciatore ch'io sappia.
Morì forse nel mezzo del mattino. E non n'ebbi
mai notizia. Suppongo che di me
abbia perduto anche il ricordo. Se ora,
qualche fantasma aleggia qui d'attorno
non posso catturarlo per chiedergli chi sei?
Può darsi che i fantasmi non abbiano più consistenza
di un breve soffio di vento. Uno di questi rèfoli
potrei essere anch'io senza saperlo: labile
al punto che la messa in scena di cartone
che mi circonda può restare in piedi.
Ben altri soffi occorrono per distruggerla.
Dove potranno allora rifugiarsi
questi errabondi veli? Non c'è scienza
filosofia teologia che se ne occupi.

[CHISSÀ]

Chissà se un giorno butteremo le maschere
che portiamo sul volto senza saperlo.
Per questo è tanto difficile identificare
gli uomini che incontriamo.
Forse fra i tanti, fra i milioni c'è
quello in cui viso e maschera coincidono
e lui solo potrebbe dirci la parola

[THE BLACKCAP]

The blackcap wasn't killed
by a hunter so far as I know.
Perhaps it died in the middle of the morning.
And I didn't hear about it.
I suppose it has forgotten all about me.
Now if some phantom flits about here
I cannot catch it to ask
who are you? It could be
that phantoms have no more substance
than a momentary breeze. Even I
could be one of those breezes without knowing it:
so ephemeral that even the cardboard staging
that surrounds me can stand up by itself.
It needs quite a different kind of breeze
to destroy it. Where then will these vagrant
phantoms be able to take refuge?
There's no science philosophy theology
that bothers about them.

[WHO KNOWS]

Who knows if one day we'll throw away the masks
we wear without knowing it.
That's why it's so difficult to identify the men
we meet. Perhaps among the many,
the millions there's one whose face
and mask coincide
and he alone can utter the word

che attendiamo da sempre. Ma è probabile
ch'egli stesso non sappia il suo privilegio.
Chi l'ha saputo, se uno ne fu mai,
pagò il suo dono con balbuzie o peggio.
Non valeva la pena di trovarlo. Il suo nome
fu sempre impronunciabile per cause
non solo di fonetica. La scienza
ha ben altro da fare o da non fare.

DA UN TACCUINO

Passano in formazioni romboidali
velocissimi altissimi gli storni
visti e scomparsi in un baleno
così fitti
che non c'è punto di luce
in quel rombo —
saranno i più duri a sopravvivere
secondo gli ornitologi ecologi
è ciò che sappiamo di loro
è poco ma è moltissimo —
magari potesse dirsi
lo stesso
delle formazioni sub erranti
vociferanti
dell'uomo.

we have always been waiting to hear.
But probably he himself doesn't know his privilege.
And if there ever was one who knew it
he paid for his gift with stammerings
or worse. It wasn't worth finding him.
His name was always unpronounceable and
not for phonetic reasons only.
Science has other things to do or not to do.

FROM A DIARY

Glimpsed and gone in a flash
the starlings pass swift and high
in rhomboidal formations so
tightly packed
that not a point of light
penetrates that rhombus—
they have the best chance of surviving
according to the ornithologists ecologists
which is all that we know about them
it's not much and yet
it's a lot—I wish one could say
the same
of the nomadic
vociferous formations
of man.

[QUESTO RIPUDIO]

Questo ripudio mio
dell'iconolatria
non si estende alla Mente
che vi è sottesa e pretesa
dagli idolatri.
Non date un volto a chi non ne possiede
perché non è una fattura.
Piuttosto vergognatevi di averne uno
e così cieco e sordo fin che dura.

[L'OMICIDIO NON È IL MIO FORTE]

L'omicidio non è il mio forte.
Di uomini nessuno, forse qualche insetto,
qualche zanzara schiacciata con una pantofola
sul muro.
Per molti anni provvidero le zanzariere
a difenderle. In seguito, per lunghissimo tempo,
divenni io stesso insetto ma indifeso.
Ho scoperto ora che vivere
non è questione di dignità o d'altra
categoria morale. Non dipende,
non dipese da noi. La dipendenza
può esaltarci talvolta, non ci rallegra mai.

[MY REPUDIATION]

My repudiation
of iconolatry
doesn't extend to the Mind
which idolaters claim is behind it.
Don't give him a face who hasn't got one
because it's not something manufactured.
Rather be ashamed of having yourself
such a blind and a deaf face
so long as it lasts.

[MURDER IS NOT MY STRONG POINT]

Murder is not my strong point.
I've never killed a man, perhaps
a few insects, some mosquitoes,
squashed with a slipper on the wall.
For many years the mosquito nets
managed to defend them. Later,
for a long time, I myself became
an insect, but a defenseless one.
I've now discovered that living
is not a question of dignity
or of any other moral category.
It doesn't depend, never did
depend on us. Dependence
may sometimes make us feel
elated, it never cheers us up.

[SIAMO ALLA SOLITUDINE DI GRUPPO]

Siamo alla solitudine di gruppo,
un fatto nuovo nella storia e certo
non il migliore a detta
di qualche Zebedeo che sta da solo.
Non sarà poi gran male. Ho qui sul tavolo
un individuo collettivo, un marmo
di coralli più duro di un macigno.
Sembra che abbia una forma definitiva,
resistente al martello. Si avvantaggia
sul banco degli umani perchè non parla.

[SE AL PIÙ SI OPPONE IL MENO]

Se al più si oppone il meno il risultato
sarà destruente. Così dicevi un giorno
mostrando rudimenti di latino
e altre nozioni. E proprio in quel momento
brillò si spense, ribrillò una luce
sull'opposta costiera. Già imbruniva.
« Anche il faro, lo vedi, è intermittente,
forse è troppo costoso tenerlo sempre acceso.
Perché ti meravigli se ti dico che tutte
le capinere hanno breve suono e sorte.
Non se ne vedono molte intorno. È aperta la caccia.
Se somigliano a me sono contate
le mie ore o i miei giorni. »
                              (E fu poi vero).

[WE HAVE NOW REACHED]

We have now reached the stage of group solitude,
a new fact in history and certainly
not the best according to some
Zebedee who remains alone
But then it may not be all that bad.
I have on the table a collective individual,
a marble of corals harder than a stone.
It seems to have a definitive form
which resists the hammer. It has
an advantage over the reef of humans
because it doesn't talk.

[IF THE LESS OPPOSE THE MORE]

If the less oppose the more,
the outcome will be disastrous. So you said
by way of explaining the rudiments
of Latin and other notions.
And just at that moment there shone
went out, shone again
a light on the opposite coast.
It was already dusk. "Even the lighthouse,
you see, is intermittent, perhaps
it costs too much to keep it always lit.
Why do you wonder if I tell you that the chirping
of all blackcaps is as brief as their fate.
There aren't many to be seen around.
The hunting season has begun.
If they are anything like me my days
or my hours are numbered."
(And it was true).

RETI PER UCCELLI

Di uccelli presi dal ròccolo
quasi note su pentagramma
ne ho tratteggiate non poche
col carboncino
e non ne ho mai dedotte conclusioni
subliminari.
Il paretaio è costituzionale,
non è subacqueo, né abissale né
può svelare alcunché di sostanziale.
Il paretaio ce lo portiamo addosso
come una spolverina. È invisibile
e non mai rammendabile perché non si cuce.
Il problema di uscirne non si pone,
che dobbiamo restarci fu deciso da altri.

DOMANDE SENZA RISPOSTA

Mi chiedono se ho scritto
un canzoniere d'amore
e se il mio onlie begetter
è uno solo o è molteplice.
Ahimè,
la mia testa è confusa, molte figure
vi si addizionano,
ne formano una sola che discerno
a malapena nel mio crepuscolo.
Se avessi posseduto
un liuto come d'obbligo
per un trobar meno chiuso

NETS FOR BIRDS

Of birds caught in the nets with decoys
almost like notes on the pentagram
I've sketched quite a few with charcoal
but I haven't drawn any subliminal conclusions
about them. The net is constitutional,
not subacqueous or abysmal, nor
can it reveal anything substantial.
We wear a net like a duster. It is
invisible and can never be mended
because it can't be sewn.
The problem of getting out of it
doesn't arise, for it was
already decided by others
that we should stay inside it.

QUESTIONS WITHOUT AN ANSWER

They ask me if I have written
a collection of love poems and
if my onlie begetter is
one or manifold.
Alas,
my head is confused, many figures
add up there, forming only
one which I barely discern
in my twilight. Had I possessed
a lute as was required of a less
hermetic troubadour it wouldn't
have been difficult to give a name

non sarebbe difficile
dare un nome a colei che ha posseduto
la mia testa poetica o altro ancora.
Se il nome
fosse una conseguenza delle cose,
di queste non potrei dirne una sola
perché le cose sono fatti e i fatti
in prospettiva sono appena cenere.
Non ho avuto purtroppo che la parola,
qualche cosa che approssima ma non tocca;
e così
non c'è depositaria del mio cuore
che non sia nella bara. Se il suo nome
fosse un nome o più nomi non conta nulla
per chi è rimasto fuori, ma per poco,
della divina inesistenza. A presto,
adorate mie larve!

VIVERE
Vivere? Lo facciano per noi i nostri domestici.
Villiers de l'Isle-Adam

I
È il tema che mi fu dato
quando mi presentai all'esame
per l'ammissione alla vita.
Folla di prenativi i candidati,
molti per loro fortuna i rimandati.
Scrissi su un foglio d'aria senza penna
e pennino, il pensiero non c'era ancora.

to her who possessed
my poetic mind and much else.
If the name
were a consequence of things
I could not mention a single one
because things are facts and facts
in perspective are barely ashes.
All I have had unfortunately
is the word, which is something that approaches
but doesn't touch;
and thus
there is no repository of my heart
who is not in the grave.
If her name was one or many
doesn't count for him who has
stayed outside of divine inexistence
but only for a while. I shall see you
soon my beloved ghosts!

LIVING
Living? Let our servants do it for us.
Villiers de l'Isle-Adam

I
This is the topic I was given when I took
my exam for admittance to life.
The examinees an unborn crowd
of whom many were lucky to have been asked
to repeat the exam. I wrote
on a sheet of air without a pen or nib,
the thought wasn't there yet. Had I

Mi fossi ricordato che Epittéto in catene
era la libertà assoluta l'avrei detto,
se avessi immaginato che la rinunzia
era il fatto più nobile dell'uomo
l'avrei scritto ma il foglio restò bianco.
Il ricordo obiettai, non anticipa, segue.

Si udì dopo un silenzio un parlottìo tra i giudici.
Poi uno d'essi mi consegnò l'accessit
e disse non t'invidio.

II
Una risposta
da terza elementare. Me ne vergogno.
Vivere non era per Villiers la vita
né l'oltrevita ma la sfera occulta
di un genio che non chiede la fanfara.
Non era in lui disprezzo per il sottobosco.
Lo ignorava, ignorava quasi tutto
e anche se stesso. Respirava l'aria
dell'Eccelso come io quella pestifera
di qui.

CABALETTA

La nostra mente sbarca
i fatti più importanti che ci occorsero
e imbarca i più risibili. Ciò prova
la deficienza dell'imbarcazione

remembered that Epictetus in chains
was absolute liberty I would have said so,
had I imagined that renunciation
was the noblest thing about man
I would have written it but the page remained blank.
Memory, I objected, doesn't anticipate, it follows.

There was a silence for a while, some muttering
among the judges. Then one of them gave me
admittance and said I don't envy you.

II
A reply
like an elementary school child's.
I'm ashamed of it. Living for Villiers
was neither life nor the afterlife
but the occult sphere of a genius
that doesn't ask for a fanfare.
He had no contempt for shady characters.
He ignored them, ignored almost everything
including himself. He breathed
the air of the Sublime as I
the pestiferous air down here.

CABALETTA

Our mind throws overboard the most
important things that happened to us
and takes on board the most ludicrous.
This shows the flaw in the boat and in him

e di chi l'ha costruita. Il Calafato
supremo non si mise mai a nostra
disposizione. È troppo affaccendato.

I PRESSEPAPIERS

Quando pubblicai Buffalo e Keepsake
un critico illustre e anche amico volse il pollice
e decretò carenza di sentimento quasi
che sentimento e ricordo fossero incompatibili.
In verità di keepsakes in senso letterale
ne posseggo ben pochi. Non ho torri pendenti
in miniatura, minigondole o simili
cianfrusaglie ma ho lampi che s'accendono
e si spengono. È tutto il mio bagaglio.
Il guaio è che il ricordo non è gerarchico,
ignora le precedenze e le susseguenze
e abbuia l'importante, ciò che ci parve tale.
Il ricordo è un lucignolo, il solo che ci resta.
C'è il caso che si stacchi e viva per conto suo.
Ciò che non fu illuminato fu corporeo, non vivo.
Abbiamo gli Dèi o anche un dio a portata di mano
senza saperne nulla. Solo i dementi acciuffano
qualche soffio. È un errore essere in terra
e lo pagano.

who constructed it. The supreme Caulker
never put himself at our disposal.
He is too busy.

THE PAPERWEIGHTS

When I published "Buffalo" and "Keepsake"
an eminent critic and friend
gave them thumbs down and decreed
that they were lacking in sentiment almost
as if sentiment and memory were incompatible.
In fact I have very few keepsakes
in the literal sense of the word.
I have no miniature leaning towers,
no mini-gondolas or other trifles;
but I have flashlights that light up and go out.
This is all the baggage I have.
The trouble is that memory is not hierarchical,
it ignores what precedes and follows
and obscures what's important, or
what seemed so to us. Memory
is a wick, the only one left us.
It might possibly detach itself
and live on its own. What was not
illumined was corporeal, not living.
We have the Gods or even a god within reach
without knowing anything about it.
Only the insane snatch at some breeze.
It is a mistake to be on earth
and they pay for it.

SUL LAGO D'ORTA

Le Muse stanno appollaiate
sulla balaustrata
appena un filo di brezza sull'acqua
c'è qualche albero illustre
la magnolia il cipresso l'ippocastano
la vecchia villa è scortecciata
da un vetro rotto vedo sofà ammuffiti
e un tavolo da ping-pong. Qui non viene nessuno
da molti anni. Un guardiano era previsto
ma si sa come vanno le previsioni.
È strana l'angoscia che si prova
in questa deserta proda sabbiosa erbosa
dove i salici piangono davvero
e ristagna indeciso tra vita e morte
un intermezzo senza pubblico. È
un'angoscia limbale sempre incerta
tra la catastrofe e l'apoteosi
di una rigogliosa decrepitudine.
Se il bandolo del puzzle più tormentoso
fosse più che un'ubbia
sarebbe strano trovarlo dove neppure un'anguilla
tenta di sopravvivere. Molti anni fa c'era qui
una famiglia inglese. Purtroppo manca il custode
ma forse quegli angeli (angli) non erano così pazzi
da essere custoditi.

ON THE LAKE OF ORTA

The Muses are roosting
on the balustrade
hardly a breath of air on the water
there are some illustrious trees
the magnolia the cypress the horse-chestnut
the old villa is peeling
through a broken window I see moldy
sofas and a Ping-Pong table.
No one has set foot here for years.
A caretaker was expected
but we all know what expectations are.
It's strange the anguish one feels
on this deserted, grassy, sandy bank
where the willows really do weep
and an intermezzo without a public
stagnates undecided between life and death.
It's a limbo-like anguish
of a vigorous decrepitude
always hovering between the catastrophe and the
    apotheosis.
If the key to the most baffling puzzle
were something more than a whim
it would be strange to find it where not even an eel
tries to survive. Many years ago
there was an English family here.
Unfortunately
the guardian is missing perhaps
those angels (Angles) were not so mad
as to be guarded.

IL FURORE

Il furore è antico quanto l'uomo
ma credeva di avere un obiettivo.
Ora basta a se stesso. È un passo avanti
ma non è sufficiente. L'uomo deve
pure restando un bipede mutarsi
in un altro animale. Solo allora
sarà come le belve a quattro zampe innocuo
se non sia aggredito. Ci vorrà
un po' d'anni o millenni. È un batter d'occhio.

[TERMINARE LA VITA]

Terminare la vita
tra le stragi e l'orrore
è potuto accadere
per l'abnorme sviluppo del pensiero
poiché il pensiero non è mai buono in sé.
Il pensiero è aberrante per natura.
Era frenato un tempo da invisibili Numi,
ora gli idoli sono in carne ed ossa
e hanno appetito. Noi siamo il loro cibo.
Il peggio dell'orrore è il suo ridicolo.
Noi crediamo di assistervi imparziali
o plaudenti e ne siamo la materia stessa.
La nostra tomba non sarà certo un'ara
ma il water di chi ha fame ma non testa.

FURY

Fury is as old as man
but it used to think it had an objective.
Now it is self-sufficient. It's a step
forward but it's not enough.
Man, while remaining a biped,
must change into another animal.
Only then will he be
like the wild four-legged beasts
harmless unless attacked.
It will take a few years or millennia.
The twinkling of an eye.

[TO END LIFE]

To end life
amidst slaughter and horror
has been possible thanks to the abnormal
development of thought since thought
is never good in itself.
Thought is aberrant by its nature. Once
invisible Deities curbed it; now
the idols are there in the flesh
and are hungry. We are their food.
The worst of the horror is
its ridiculous side. We think
we are merely impartial spectators who applaud
and we are the play itself.
Our tomb won't be
an altar but the W.C. of him
who has hunger but no head.

APPUNTI

Sarà una fine dolcissima
in *ppp*
dopodiché ci troveremo
sprovvisti di memoria
con anima incorporea
stordita come mai e timorosa
d'altri guai.

*

Ahura Mazra e Arimane
il mio pensiero persiano
di stamane

. . .

e noi poveri bastardi
figli di cani
abbassata la cresta
attenti disattenti a uno spettacolo
che non ci riguarda

*

GINA ALL'ALBA MI DICE

il merlo è sulla frasca
e dondola
felice.

GLI ELEFANTI

I due elefanti hanno seppellito con cura
il loro elefantino.
Hanno coperto di foglie la sua tomba e poi

NOTES

The end will be very sweet
in *ppp*
after which we shall find ourselves
deprived of memory with
an incorporeal soul dazed as never before
and fearing other troubles.
*

Ahura Mazdah and Ahriman
my Persian thought
of this morning
. . .
and we poor bastards
sons of bitches
having come off our high horses
attentive and inattentive to a show
that doesn't concern us
*

GINA TELLS ME AT DAWN

the blackbird is on the branch
and is swinging
happily.

THE ELEPHANTS

The two elephants have buried with care
their little one. Have
covered his tomb with leaves

si sono allontanati tristemente.
Vicino a me qualcuno si asciugò un ciglio.
Era davvero una furtiva lacrima
quale la pietà chiede quando è inerme:
in proporzione inversa alla massiccia
imponenza del caso. Gli altri ridevano
perché qualche buffone era già apparso
sullo schermo.

L'EUFORIA

Se l'euforia può essere la più tetra
apertura sul mondo
amici che subsannate
alla mia ottusa inappartenenza . . .
a chi? a che cosa? posso dirvi che
se resterà una corda alla mia cetra
avrò meglio di voi e senza occhiali
affumicati la mia vita in rosa.

EPIGRAMMA

Il vertice lo zenit
il summit, il cacume,
o Numi
chi mai li arresta.

E c'è chi si stupisce
se qualcuno si butta
dalla finestra.

and have sadly gone away.
Someone beside me wiped his eye.
It was really a furtive tear
such as pity calls forth when it is unarmed:
in inverse proportion to the massive
bulk of the case. The others were laughing
because some buffoon had already
appeared on the screen.

EUPHORIA

If euphoria can be the darkest
opening on to the world
friends who sneer at my
obtuse unbelongingness . . .
to whom? to what? I can tell you
that if a string is still left on my zither
I shall have more than you and without tinted glasses
a rosy life for me.

EPIGRAM

Vertex zenith
summit, acme
O Gods
who can ever stop them.

And there are those who are amazed
if someone throws himself
out of the window.

IN NEGATIVO

È strano.
Sono stati sparati colpi a raffica
su di noi e il ventaglio non mi ha colpito.
Tuttavia avrò presto il mio benservito
forse in carta da bollo da presentare
chissà a quale burocrate; ed è probabile
che non occorra altro. Il peggio è già passato.
Ora sono superflui i documenti, ora
è superfluo anche il meglio. Non c'è stato
nulla, assolutamente nulla dietro di noi,
e nulla abbiamo disperatamente amato più di quel
    nulla.

LA CULTURA

Se gli ardenti bracieri di Marcione e di Ario
avessero arrostito gli avversari
(ma fu vero il contrario)
il mondo avrebbe scritto la parola fine
per sopraggiunta infungibilità.

Così disse uno che si forbì gli occhiali
e poi sparò due colpi.
Un uccello palustre cadde a piombo.
Solo una piuma restò sospesa in aria.

IN THE NEGATIVE

It's strange.
A burst of shots was fired at us
and the blast hasn't struck me.
However I shall soon be given
the sack perhaps on stamped paper to be presented
to who knows what bureaucrat; and probably
nothing else will be needed.
The worst is already over. Now
the documents are all superfluous, and so also
is the best. There has been nothing,
absolutely nothing behind us,
and we have loved nothing so desperately as
    that nothing.

CULTURE

If the glowing braziers of Marcion and Arius
had roasted their enemies
(but the contrary was true)
the world would have written the word end
and in addition irreplaceable.

So said someone as he wiped his glasses
and then fired two shots.
A fen-bird fell plumb.
Only a feather remained suspended in the air.

IN UNA CITTÀ DEL NORD

Come copia dell'Eden primigenio
manca il confronto con l'originale.
Certo vale qualcosa. Gli scoiattoli
saltano su trapezi di rami alti.
Rari i bambini, ognuno di più padri o madri.
Anche se non fa freddo c'è aria di ghiacciaia.
A primavera si dovrà difendersi
dalle volpi o da altre bestie da pelliccia.
Così mi riferisce il mio autista
navarrese o gallego portato qui dal caso.
Non gli va giù la democrácia. Tale
e quale il Marqués de Villanova.
Io guardo e penso o fingo. Si paga a caro prezzo
un'anima moderna. Potrei anche provarmici.

DI UN GATTO SPERDUTO

Il povero orfanello
non s'era ancora inselvatichito
se fu scacciato dal condominio
perché non lacerasse le moquettes con gli unghielli.
Me ne ricordo ancora passando per quella via
dove accaddero fatti degni di storia
ma indegni di memoria. Fors'è che qualche briciola
voli per conto suo.

IN A NORTHERN CITY

Like a copy of primeval Eden
the comparison with the original is missing.
It's worth something no doubt. The squirrels
leap on to the trapezes of high branches.
There are very few children, each
with more than one father or mother.
Even if it isn't cold the air is icy.
In spring one will have to defend oneself
from the foxes or other furry animals.
So says my chauffeur from Navarre or Galicia
brought over here by chance.
He can't swallow democrácia.
Just like the Marqués de Villanova.
I look out and think or pretend to.
One pays dearly for a modern soul.
I too might try one.

ON A STRAY CAT

The poor little stray
had not yet turned wild even though
thrown out from the block of flats
for fear he might tear the carpet with his claws.
I still remember him as I pass through the street
which saw events worthy of history
but not worth remembering. Perhaps
some crumb might fly of its own accord.

IPOTESI

Nella valle di Armageddon
Iddio e il diavolo conversano
pacificamente dei loro affari.
Nessuno dei due ha interesse
a uno scontro decisivo.
L'Apocalissi sarebbe
da prendersi con le molle?
È più che certo ma questo
non può insegnarsi nelle scuole.
Io stesso fino da quando
ero alunno delle elementari
credevo di essere un combattente
dalla parte giusta.
Gli insegnanti erano miti, non frustavano.
Gli scontri erano posti nell'ovatta,
incruenti, piacevoli. Il peggio
era veduto in prospettiva. Quello
che più importava era che il soccombente
fosse dall'altra parte.
Così passarono gli anni, troppi e inutili.
Fu sparso molto sangue che non fecondò i campi.
Eppure la parte giusta era lì, a due palmi
e non fu mai veduta. Fosse mai accaduto
il miracolo nulla era più impossibile
dell'esistenza stessa di noi uomini.
Per questo nella valle di Armageddon
non accadono mai risse e tumulti.

HYPOTHESIS

In the valley of Armageddon
God and the devil converse
peacefully about their affairs.
Neither is interested in
a decisive conflict.
Will the Apocalypse have to be handled
with kid gloves?
It's more than certain but this
cannot be taught in the schools.
I myself since my primary schooldays
thought I was fighting on the right side.
The teachers were kind, they didn't cane us.
Conflicts were muffled in cotton wool,
quite bloodless, pleasant. The worst
was seen in perspective. What mattered most
was that the loser was on the other side.
Thus years passed, too many and useless.
Much blood was shed which didn't fertilize the
    fields.
And yet the right side was there, just two
steps away and it was never seen.
Had the miracle ever happened
nothing would have been more impossible
than the very existence of us men.
Hence in the valley of Armageddon
there are never any fights or riots.

AI TUOI PIEDI

Mi sono inginocchiato ai tuoi piedi
o forse è un'illusione perché non si vede
nulla di te
ed ho chiesto perdono per i miei peccati
attendendo il verdetto con scarsa fiducia
e debole speranza non sapendo
che senso hanno quassù il prima e il poi
il presente il passato l'avvenire
e il fatto che io sia venuto al mondo
senza essere consultato.
Poi penserò alla vita di quaggiù
non sub specie aeternitatis,
non risalendo all'infanzia
e agli ingloriosi fatti che l'hanno illustrata
per poi ascendere a un dopo
di cui sarò all'anteporta.
Attendendo il verdetto
che sarà lungo o breve grato o ingrato
ma sempre temporale e qui comincia
l'imbroglio perché nulla di buono è mai pensabile
nel tempo,
ricorderò gli oggetti che ho lasciati
al loro posto, un posto tanto studiato,
agli uccelli impagliati, a qualche ritaglio
di giornale, alle tre o quattro medaglie
di cui sarò derubato e forse anche
alle fotografie di qualche mia Musa
che mai seppe di esserlo,
rifarò il censimento di quel nulla

AT YOUR FEET

I have knelt at your feet,
or perhaps it's an illusion, for one
cannot see you, and I have asked
pardon for my sins
while awaiting
the verdict without much faith
and little hope not knowing what sense
before and after, present past
future have up there
and the fact that I came into the world
without being consulted.
I shall then think of the life down here,
not under the cloak of eternity,
nor going back to childhood,
and the inglorious facts that characterized it,
in order to ascend to an afterwards
and be at its outer door. Awaiting
the verdict whether long or short,
favorable or unfavorable but always
temporal and that's the catch,
for nothing good is ever thinkable
within time, I shall remember the objects
I left in their place, a carefully chosen place,
amidst the stuffed birds, some newspaper cuttings
three or four medals of which
I shall be robbed and perhaps
also the photographs of some of my Muses
who never knew they were such,
I shall again take the census of that

che fu vivente perché fu tangibile
e mi dirò se non fossero
queste solo e non altro la mia consistenza
e non questo corpo ormai incorporeo
che sta in attesa e quasi si addormenta.

CHI È IN ASCOLTO

Tra i molti profeti barbati che girano intorno
qualcuno avrà anche toccato la verità
ma l'ha toccata col dito e poi l'ha ritratto.
La verità scotta.
Il più che possa dirsi è appunto che
se può farsene a meno
questo è voluto da chi non può
fare a meno di noi.
Forse è una botta per tutti
e non motivo di orgoglio.
Se colui che ci ha posto in questa sede
può talvolta lavarsene le mani
ciò vuol dire che Arimane
è all'attacco e non cede.

LE ORE DELLA SERA

Dovremo attendere un pezzo prima che la cronaca
si camuffi in storia.
Solo allora il volo di una formica

nothing which was living because
it was tangible and I shall ask myself
if only these constituted my substance
and nothing else,
not this body incorporeal by now
which while waiting almost falls asleep.

HE WHO IS LISTENING

Amongst the many bearded prophets wandering
    around
someone might even have touched the truth but only
with his finger which he then withdrew.
The truth burns.
The most one can say is
that if one can do without it
it is something willed by him
who cannot do without us.
Perhaps it's a blow for everyone
and not a reason for pride.
If he who put us in this place can at times
wash his hands of us it means
that Ahriman is on the offensive
and won't give in.

THE EVENING HOURS

We shall have to wait quite a while
before the news is camouflaged as history.
Only then will the flight of an ant

(il solo che interessi) sarà d'aquila.
Solo allora il fischietto del pipistrello
ci parrà la trombetta del dies irae.
Il fatto è che ci sono i baccalaureandi
e bisogna cacciarli tutti in qualche buco
per scacciarneli poi se verrà il bello.
Purtroppo il bello (o brutto) è in frigorifero
né si vede chi voglia o possa trarnelo fuori.
Il pipistrello stride solo al crepuscolo
di ciò che un tempo si diceva il giorno
ma ormai non abbiamo più giornate,
siamo tutti una nera colata indivisibile
che potrebbe arrestarsi
o farsi scolaticcio non si sa
con vantaggio di chi.

LA VERITÀ

La verità è nei rosicchiamenti
delle tarme e dei topi,
nella polvere ch'esce da cassettoni ammuffiti
e nelle croste dei « grana » stagionati.
La verità è la sedimentazione, il ristagno,
non la logorrea schifa dei dialettici.
È una tela di ragno, può durare,
non distruggetela con la scopa.
È beffa di scoliasti l'idea che tutto si muova,
l'idea che dopo un prima viene un dopo

(the only one of interest)
be that of an eagle. Only then
will the squeak of the bat seem to us
like the trumpet of the *Dies Irae*.
The fact is that there are the would-be baccalaureates
whom we must drive
into some hole to drive them out again
if better times come.
Unfortunately the better (or worse)
is in the fridge and one can't see
who wants it or who can bring it out.
The bat screeches only in the dusk
of what was once called the day,
but now we no longer have days,
we are all a black indivisible molten
mass that might stop or turn into dross
nobody knows to whose advantage.

THE TRUTH

The truth lies in the nibblings
of moths and mice,
in the powder that issues from moldy
chests of drawers, in the crusts
of seasoned Parmesan.
The truth is sedimentation, stagnation, not
the nauseating ravings of dialectics.
It's a spider's web, it can last,
don't destroy it with the broom.
The idea that everything moves

fa acqua da tutte le parti. Salutiamo
gli inetti che non s'imbarcano. Si starà meglio
senza di loro, si starà anche peggio
ma si tirerà il fiato.

NEL DISUMANO

Non è piacevole
saperti sottoterra anche se il luogo
può somigliare a un'Isola dei Morti
con un sospetto di Rinascimento.
Non è piacevole a pensarsi ma
il peggio è nel vedere. Qualche cipresso,
tombe di second'ordine con fiori finti,
fuori un po' di parcheggio per improbabili
automezzi. Ma so che questi morti
abitavano qui a due passi, tu
sei stata un'eccezione. Mi fa orrore
che quello ch'è lì dentro, quattro ossa
e un paio di gingilli fu creduto il tutto
di te e magari lo era, atroce a dirsi.
Forse partendo in fretta hai creduto
che chi si muove prima trova il posto migliore.
Ma quale posto e dove? Si continua
a pensare con teste umane quando si entra
nel disumano.

is the annotators' hoax, the idea
that after a before comes an after
is letting in water on every side.
Let's salute the inept who don't embark.
We'll be better off without them, we might even
be worse off but at least
we shall draw breath.

THE INHUMAN

It isn't pleasant
to know that you are under the earth
even if the place is like an Island of the Dead
with a suggestion of Renaissance. It isn't
pleasant to think about it
but it's worse to see. A few cypresses,
second-rate tombs with artificial
flowers, and outside a small
parking lot for improbable
vehicles. But I know
that these dead lived a few steps from here,
you were an exception. I am
horrified to think that what's inside,
four bones and a few trinkets was
believed to be all of you
and perhaps it was, though it's terrible to say so.
Maybe you left in a hurry thinking
that he who makes the first move
gets the best place. But what place
and where? One continues to think
with a human head while entering the inhuman.

GLI ANIMALI

Gli animali di specie più rara
prossima a estinguersi
destano costernazione
in chi sospetta che il loro Padre ne abbia
perduto lo stampino.

Non è che tutti siano stati vittime
degli uomini e dei climi
o di un artefice divino.
Chi li ha creati li ha creduti inutili
al più infelice dei suoi prodotti: noi.

L'OBBROBRIO

Non fatemi discendere amici cari
fino all'ultimo gradino
della poesia sociale.
Se l'uno è poca cosa il collettivo
è appena frantumazione
e polvere, niente di più.
Se l'emittente non dà che borborigmi
che ne sarà dei recipienti? Solo
supporre che ne siano, immaginare
che il più contenga il meno, che un'accozzaglia
sia una totalità,
nulla di ciò fu creduto nei grandi secoli
che rimpiangiamo perché non ci siamo nati
e per nostra fortuna ci è impossibile
retrocedere.

THE ANIMALS

The animals of the rarest species
which is on the verge of extinction
arouse consternation in those who suspect
that their Father has lost the mold.

It's not that they were all victims
of men or climates or
of a divine craftsman. He
who made them thought they were useless
to the unhappiest of his products: us.

OPPROBRIUM

Friends don't make me come down
to the lowest step of the social
ladder of poetry. If
one step is a paltry thing,
all steps collectively are
dust and fragmentation,
nothing more.
If the emitter emits only borborygms
then what will become of the recipients?
Only to suppose that there are any,
imagine that the more contains
the less, and that a disorderly mass
is totality, nothing of this
was believed in the great centuries we miss
because we weren't born in them
and luckily for us it is
impossible to go back.

RIBALTAMENTO

La vasca è un grande cerchio, vi si vedono
ninfee e pesciolini rosa pallido.
Mi sporgo e vi cado dentro ma dà l'allarme
un bimbo della mia età.
Chissà se c'è ancora acqua. Curvo il braccio
e tocco il pavimento della mia stanza.

QUEL CHE RESTA (SE RESTA)

la vecchia serva analfabeta
e barbuta chissà dov'è sepolta
poteva leggere il mio nome e il suo
come ideogrammi
forse non poteva riconoscersi
neppure allo specchio
ma non mi perdeva d'occhio
della vita non sapendone nulla
ne sapeva più di noi
nella vita quello che si acquista
da una parte si perde dall'altra
chissà perché la ricordo
più di tutto e di tutti
se entrasse ora nella mia stanza
avrebbe centotrent'anni e griderei di spavento.

OVERTURNING

The basin is a large circle in which
one can see nymphs and little pale pink fish.
I stretch out and fall into it but
a child of my age raises the alarm.
Who knows if there's still water in it. I bend
my arm and touch the floor of my room.

THAT WHICH REMAINS (IF IT DOES)

the old illiterate bearded
maidservant who knows where she is buried
she could read her name and mine
as ideograms
perhaps she couldn't recognize herself
even in the mirror
but she never lost sight of me
and while not knowing anything about life
she knew more than we
what one acquires in life on the one hand
one loses on the other
who knows why I remember her
more than anything or anybody else
if she were to enter my room now she would be
one hundred and thirty and I would cry out in fright.

LA POESIA
(In Italia)

Dagli albori del secolo si discute
se la poesia sia dentro o fuori.
Dapprima vinse il dentro, poi contrattaccò
    duramente
il fuori e dopo anni si addivenne a un forfait
che non potrà durare perché il fuori
è armato fino ai denti.

UN SOGNO, UNO DEI TANTI

Il sogna che si ripete è che non ricordo più
il mio indirizzo e corro per rincasare
È notte, la valigia che porto è pesante
e mi cammina accanto un Arturo
molto introdotto in ville di famose lesbiane
e anche lui reputato per i tanti suoi meriti
Vorrebbe certo soccorrermi in tale congiuntura
ma mi fa anche notare che non ha tempo da perdere
Egli abita a sinistra io tiro per la destra
ma non so se sia giusta la strada il numero la città
Anche il nome m'è dubbio, quello di chi attualmente
mi ospita padre fratello parente più o meno lontano
mi frulla vorticoso nella mente, vi si affaccia persino
un tavolo una poltrona una barba di antenato
l'intera collezione di un'orrenda rivista teatrale
le dieci o dodici rampe di scale dove una zia
    d'acquisto

POETRY
In Italy

Since the beginning of the century
we have been discussing whether poetry is inner
or outer. At first the inner won,
then the outer counterattacked furiously
and after years they have come to an agreement
which won't last for the outer is
armed to the teeth.

A DREAM, ONE OF MANY

A recurrent dream of mine is that I've forgotten
my address and I run to get home
It's night, the suitcase I'm carrying is heavy
and a certain Arthur is walking beside me
he's quite popular in the villas of famous lesbians
and he too is known for his many virtues
He would of course like to help me in such a pass
but at the same time he points out that
he hasn't got any time to waste
He lives on the left I'm moving towards the right
but I don't know if the number the street the city
are right I'm even doubtful as to the name
of my present host father brother
or a more or less distant relative
the name whirls giddily in my mind,
there even appears a table an armchair an ancestor's
    beard

fu alzata tra le braccia di un cattivo tenore
e giurò da quel giorno che gli ascensori erano inutili
a donne del suo rango e delle sue forme
(invero spaventevoli) tutto mi è vivo e presente
fuorché la porta a cui potrò bussare
senza sentirmi dire vada a farsi f-
Forse potrei tentare da un apposito chiosco
un telefonico approccio ma dove trovare il gettone
e a quale numero poi? mentre che Arturo si scusa
e dice che di troppo si è allontanato dalla
sua via del Pellegrino di cui beato lui ha ricordo
Lo strano è che in tali frangenti non mi dico mai
come il vecchio profeta Enrico lo Spaventacchio
che il legno del mio rocchetto mostra il bianco
e non avranno senso i miei guai anagrafici e
    residenziali.
Mi seggo su un paracarro o sulla pesante valigia
in attesa che si apra nel buio una porticina
e che una voce mi dica entri pure si paga anticipato
troverà la latrina nel ballatoio al terzo piano
svolti a destra poi giri a sinistra Ma di qui
comincia appena il risveglio

the complete set of a ghastly theater review
the ten or twelve flights of stairs
where an acquired aunt was lifted up in the arms
of a bad tenor and from that day on she swore
that elevators were useless to women of her rank
and proportion (really terrifying)
everything is alive and present for me
except the door at which I shall knock
without hearing someone tell me to go and get lost
Perhaps from a booth nearby I'd be able to make
a telephonic approach but where to find a coin
and what number to dial? while Arthur excuses
    himself
and says he has come too far from his Pilgrim's road
which lucky fellow he remembers
The strange thing is that at such a juncture
I never tell myself like the old prophet
Enrico the Scarecrow that the wood of my spool
is showing white and that my registrational and
    residential
difficulties won't make any sense
I sit on a wayside post or on the heavy suitcase
waiting for a door to open in the darkness
and for a voice to tell me to come in
that the room must be paid for in advance
that I shall find the toilet on the corridor
of the third floor if I turn right then left
But just at this point I begin to wake up

SCOMPARSA DELLE STRIGI

Un figlio di Minerva
ancora inetto al volo si arruffava
sul cornicione
Poi cadde nel cortile Ci mettemmo
in cerca di becchime ma inutilmente
Occorrevano vermi non sementi
Eravamo sospesi
tra pietà e ammirazione
Ci guardava con grandi occhi incredibili
Poi restò una pallottola di piume
e nient'altro
Un povero orfanello disse uno
Noi l'abbiamo scampata
se con vantaggio o no è da vedere

LE PROVE GENERALI

Qualche poeta ha voluto
praticando le prove respiratorie
di una sapienza indiana multimillenaria
procurarsi uno stato di vitamorte
che parrebbe la prova generale
di ciò che sarebbe di noi quando cadrà la tela.
Le prove generali sono la parodia
dell'intero spettacolo se mai dovremo
vederne alcuno prima di sparire
nel più profondo nulla. A meno che
le idee di tutto e nulla, di io e di non io
non siano che bagagli da buttarsi via

THE DISAPPEARANCE OF THE SCREECH OWLS

A son of Minerva
as yet inept at flying
ruffled its feathers on the ledge
Then fell into the courtyard
We looked round for birdseed but in vain
What was needed was worms not seeds
We were torn between pity and admiration
It looked at us with incredibly big eyes
Then it turned into a ball of feathers
nothing more
A poor little orphan someone said
We saved it whether for good
or ill remains to be seen

GENERAL PROOFS

By practising the breathing exercises
of multi-millennial Indian wisdom
some poets wanted to achieve
a state of life-in-death
which would seem to be the general proof
of what will become of us when the curtain falls.
The general proofs are the parody
of the whole spectacle if we should
ever see any before disappearing
into the profoundest nothing. Unless
ideas of everything and nothing,
of ego and non-ego are merely

(ma senza urgenza!) quando sia possibile
(augurabile mai) di rinunziarvi.
Pure rendiamo omaggio ai nuovi Guru
anche se dal futuro ci divide
un filo ch'è un abisso e non vogliamo
che la conocchia si assottigli troppo . . .

SENZA PERICOLO

Il filosofo interdisciplinare
è quel tale che ama *se vautrer*
(vuol dire stravaccarsi) nel più fetido
lerciume consumistico. E il peggio è
che lo fa con suprema voluttà
e ovviamente dall'alto di una cattedra
già da lui disprezzata.
              Non s'era visto mai
che un naufrago incapace di nuotare
delirasse di gioia mentre la nave
colava a picco. Ma non c'è pericolo
per gli uomini pneumatici e lui lo sa.

QUELLA DEL FARO

Suppongo che tu sia passata
senza lasciare tracce. Sono certo

baggage to be thrown away
(but without any urgency!) whenever
it is possible (with any luck never)
to renounce them. However let's pay homage
to the new gurus although a mere thread
divides us from the future—a thread
which is an abyss and we don't want
too little of it on the bobbin . . .

WITHOUT DANGER

The interdisciplinary philosopher
is the type who loves *se vautrer*
(that is to wallow) in the most
fetid consumer filth.
And the worst of it is
that he does so with supreme voluptuousness
and obviously from the height of a chair
he despises.
              One had never seen
a shipwrecked man incapable of swimming
delirious with joy while the ship
foundered. But there's no danger
for pneumatic men and he knows it.

THE WOMAN OF THE LIGHTHOUSE

I suppose you passed away
without leaving any trace. I am sure

che il tuo nome era scritto altrove, non so dove.
È un segno di elezione, il più ambito
e il più sicuro, il meno intelligibile
da chi ha in tasca un brevetto a garanzia
di « un posto al mondo » (che farebbe ridere
anche te dove sei, se ancora sei).

DALL'ALTRA SPONDA

Sebbene illetterata fu per noi
una piuma dell'aquila bicefala
questa Gerti che ormai si rifà viva
ogni morte di papa.
Un pezzo di cultura? Un'ascendenza
o solo fumo e cenere?
                    Interrogata
si dichiarò in maiuscolo ANTENATA.
Ma come la mettiamo se al tempo degli oroscopi
parve del tutto implume?

[L'IMMANE FARSA UMANA]

L'immane farsa umana
(non mancheranno ragioni per occuparsi
del suo risvolto tragico)
non è affar mio. Pertanto
mi sono rifugiato nella zona intermedia
che può chiamarsi inedia accidia o altro.

that your name was written elsewhere, I don't know
    where.
It's a sign of being elect, the most coveted
and the surest, the least intelligible
to him who has a patent in his pocket
guaranteeing "a place in the world"
(which would make even you laugh wherever
you are, if you still are).

FROM THE OTHER BANK

Although illiterate
this Gerti who now shows up once
in a blue moon was for us
a feather from the two-headed eagle.
A piece of culture? A lineage
or merely smoke and ashes?
                              Questioned
she declared in block capitals ANCESTRESS.
But how to explain it if at the time of the horoscopes
she seemed to be completely featherless?

[THE APPALLING HUMAN FARCE]

The appalling human farce
(there's no lack of reasons for dealing
with its tragic aspect) is not
my business. Hence I've taken refuge
in the intermediate zone one might call boredom
sloth or something else.

Si dirà: sei colui che cadde dal predellino
e disse poco male tanto dovevo scendere.
Ma non è così facile distinguere
discesa da caduta, cattiva sorte o mala.
Ho tentato più volte di far nascere
figure umane angeli salvifici
anche se provvisori; e se uno falliva
né si reggeva più sul piedistallo
pronta e immancabile anche la sostituta
adusata alla parte per vocazione innata
di essere il *doppio* sempre pronto al decollo
alle prime avvisaglie e a volte tale
da onnubilare dell'originale
volto falcata riso pianto tutto
ciò che conviene al calco più perfetto
di chi sembrò vivente e fu nessuno.

[LA VITA OSCILLA]

La vita oscilla
tra il sublime e l'immondo
con qualche propensione
per il secondo.
Ne sapremo di più
dopo le ultime elezioni
che si terranno lassù
o laggiù o in nessun luogo

One might say: you are one who fell
from the footstool and remarked no harm done
I had to get down anyway.
But it's not so easy to distinguish
a descent from a fall, a mishap
or misfortune. I've tried
more than once to create
human figures saving angels if only
for the time being; and if one failed
or could no longer stay on the pedestal
there was also the substitute waiting without fail
and used to the part by virtue
of an inborn vocation for being
the *double* always ready for the takeoff
for the first skirmishes
and at times even capable
of eclipsing the original's face
stride laughter weeping everything
that makes up the most perfect cast
of him who seemed living and was nobody.

[LIFE OSCILLATES]

Life oscillates between
the sublime and the filthy
with a certain propensity for the second.
We shall know more about it
after the last elections
to be held up there
or down there or nowhere
because we are all already

perché siamo già eletti
tutti quanti
e chi non lo fu
sta assai meglio quaggiù
e quando se ne accorge
è troppo tardi
les jeux sont faits
dice il croupier per l'ultima volta
e il suo cucchiaione
spazza le carte.

FINE DI SETTEMBRE

Il canto del rigògolo
è un suono d'ordinaria amministrazione
Non fa pensare al canto degli altri uccelli
Sto qui in una mezz'ombra Per alzare la tenda
si tira una funicella Ma oggi è troppa fatica
anche questo È tempo di siccità
universale, le rondini inferocite
sono pericolose Così vocifera
la radio delle vicine allevatrici di gatti
e pappagalli Di fuori sfrecciano macchine
ma non fanno rumore, solo un ronzìo un sottofondo
al martellìo vocale del rigògolo
Molta gente dev'essere sulla spiaggia
in quest'ultimo ponte di fine settimana
Se tiro la funicella eccola là
formicolante in prospettiva Quanto tempo è passato
da quando mi attendevo colpi di scena
resurrezioni e miracoli a ogni giro di sole

elected and he who wasn't
is much better off down here
and when he realizes this it's too late
les jeux sont faits
says the croupier for the last time
and his rake sweeps away the cards.

END OF SEPTEMBER

The oriole's song is a sound in the ordinary
run of things It doesn't
make one think of the song of other birds
I'm here in half shade One pulls
a cord to draw the curtain But today
even that's too tiring It is
the time of universal drought,
the ferocious swallows are dangerous
So blurts out the radio of the nearby
breeders of cats and parrots
Outside cars flash past
without making any noise, just
a buzz a background music to the oriole's
vocal hammering Many people
must be at the seaside during
this last long weekend holiday
If I pull the cord there they are swarming
in perspective How much time

Sapevo bene che il tempo era veloce
ma era una nozione scritta nei libri
Sotto lo scorrimento temporale
era la stasi che vinceva il giuoco
era un'infinitudine popolata
ricca di sé, non di uomini, divina
perché il divino non è mai parcellare
Solo ora comprendo che il tempo è duro, metallico
è un'incudine che sprizza le sue scintille
su noi povere anime ma svolge il suo lavoro
con un'orrenda indifferenza a volte
un po' beffarda come ora il canto
del rigògolo il solo dei piumati
che sa farsi ascoltare in giorni come questi

[NON È ANCORA PROVATO]

Non è ancora provato che i morti
vogliano resuscitare.
A volte li sentiamo accanto a noi
perché questa è la loro eredità.
Non è gran cosa, un gesto una parola
eppure non spiega nulla
dire che sono scherzi della memoria.
La nostra testa è labile, non può contenere
molto di ciò che fu, di ciò che è o che sarà;
la nostra testa è debole, fa un'immane fatica

has passed since I expected the *coups de théâtre*
resurrections and miracles at
each revolution of the sun
I knew well that time was swift
but it was a bookish notion
Under the flux of time
it was stasis that won the game
it was a populated infinitude rich
in itself, not in men, divine
because the divine is never split into particles
Only now I understand that time
is hard, metallic an anvil
that spits its sparks over us poor souls
but carries out its work with a horrible
indifference which is at times
rather laughable like the oriole's song now
the only bird that can make itself heard
in days like these

[IT HAS NOT YET BEEN PROVEN]

It has not yet been proven
that the dead want to come back to life.
At times we feel them by our side
because this is their inheritance.
It's not much, a gesture a word
and yet to say they are tricks of memory
explains nothing. Our head's unsteady,
it can't contain much of what was
is or will be; our head
is weak, it makes an enormous

per catturare il più e il meglio di un ectoplasma
che fu chiamato vita e che per ora
non ha un nome migliore.

SULLA SPIAGGIA

Un punto bianco in fuga
sul filo dell'orizzonte.
Un trimarano forse o altra simile zattera.
Un passo avanti nell'arte di tali barchi,
e indubbiamente anche un passo addietro.
È il passo che più affascina certi linguisti pazzi.
Si volle ridiscendere fino al secolo d'oro,
al Trecento, al Cavalca, chi più se ne ricorda.
Lo voleva un abate, commenta un bagnante erudito,
tale che restò a mezza via anche nell'iter ecclesiale.
Abate, solo abate e anche un po' giacobino.
I primi goccioloni bucano la sabbia.
Bisognerà mettere al riparo
i pattini, i gommoni, chiudere gli ombrelloni.
L'erudito bagnante si accomiata
preannunziando ulteriori noiosissime chiose.
È un fuggi fuggi, il cielo è oscuro ma
la tempesta rinvia il suo precoce sforzo.
Resta il catamarano (?) solo uccello di mare
nel quasi totale deficit dei cormorani.

effort to capture the most and the best
of an ectoplasm which was called life
and which for the moment has no better name.

ON THE BEACH

A white point in flight
on the horizon's rim.
Perhaps a trimaran or some other barge.
A step forward in the art of such boats
and no doubt also a step backward.
It's this step which most fascinates
certain crazy linguists. Some wanted
to go back to the golden age,
to the fourteenth century, to Cavalca,
and who remembers him anymore.
An abbot wanted it, comments an erudite bather,
so much that he remained halfway even in the *iter
ecclesiale.*
An abbot, only an abbot and also
something of a Jacobin. The first
big raindrops puncture the sand.
One will have to put away the "pattinos,"
the rubber rafts, and close the umbrellas.
The erudite bather takes leave promising
further boring exegetical comments.
There is a stampede, the sky's overcast
but the storm puts off its premature
fury. The catamaran (?) remains
the only seabird in the almost total
deficit of cormorants.

[SI APRONO VENATURE PERICOLOSE]

Si aprono venature pericolose
sulla crosta del mondo
è questione di anni o di secoli
e non riguarda solo la California
(ciò che ci parrebbe il minore dei guai
perché il male degli altri non ci interessa)
e noi qui stiamo poveri dementi
a parlare del cumulo dei redditi,
del compromesso storico e di altre
indegne fanfaluche. Eppure a scuola
ci avevano insegnato che il reale
e il razionale sono le due facce
della stessa medaglia!

[CI SI RIVEDE]

Ci si rivede mi disse qualcuno
prima d'infilarsi nell'aldilà.
Ma di costui non rammento niente
che faccia riconoscerne l'identità.
Laggiù/lassù non ci saranno tessere
di riconoscimento, non discorsi opinioni
appuntamenti o altrettali futilità.
Lassù/laggiù nemmeno troveremo
il Nulla e non è poco. Non avremo
né l'etere né il fuoco.

[DANGEROUS VEINS ARE OPENING]

Dangerous veins are opening
in the crust of the earth
it's a question of years or centuries
and it doesn't concern only California
(which would be the least of our worries
since the misfortunes of others don't interest us)
and here we poor fools are
talking about joint incomes, the historic compromise
and other worthless trifles.
And yet at school they had taught us
that the real and the rational are
two sides of the same coin!

[WE'LL MEET AGAIN]

We'll meet again someone told me
before slipping into the hereafter.
But I don't remember anything of him
to help me recall his identity.
Down there/up there there won't be
identity cards, speeches, opinions,
appointments or other such futilities.
Up there/down there we won't even find
Nothingness and it's no small thing.
We shall have neither ether nor fire.

AL MARE (O QUASI)

L'ultima cicala stride
sulla scorza gialla dell'eucalipto
i bambini raccolgono pinòli
indispensabili per la galantina
un cane alano urla dall'inferriata
di una villa ormai disabitata
le ville furono costruite dai padri
ma i figli non le hanno volute
ci sarebbe spazio per centomila terremotati
di qui non si vede nemmeno la proda
se può chiamarsi così quell'ottanta per cento
ceduta in uso ai bagnini
e sarebbe eccessivo pretendervi
una pace alcionica
il mare è d'altronde infestato
mentre i rifiuti in totale
formano ondulate collinette plastiche
esaurite le siepi hanno avuto lo sfratto
i deliziosi figli della ruggine
gli scriccioli o reatini come spesso
li citano i poeti E c'è anche qualche boccio
di magnolia l'etichetta di un pediatra
ma qui i bambini volano in bicicletta
e non hanno bisogno delle sue cure
Chi vuole respirare a grandi zaffate
la musa del nostro tempo la precarietà
può passare di qui senza affrettarsi
è il colpo secco quello che fa orrore
non già l'evanescenza il dolce afflato del nulla

AT THE SEASIDE (OR ALMOST)

The last cicada chirps
on the yellow bark of the eucalyptus
the children gather pine seeds
indispensable for the galantine
a bulldog barks from behind the railings
of a villa now deserted
the villas were built by the fathers
but the sons didn't want them
there would be room enough for a hundred thousand
earthquake victims from here
you can't even see the beach
if you can call it such with eighty percent of it
fallen into the hands of the proprietors
of bathhouses and it would be too much to expect
a halcyon peace there moreover
the sea is infested while the mass
of rubbish forms undulating plastic dunes
the hedges being threadbare the wrens
little birds or delicious children of rust
as the poets often call them have been evicted
And there are also some buds of magnolia
a pediatrician's card but here
the children run about on bicycles
and have no need of his attention
Whoever wants to imbibe in great whiffs
precariousness the muse of our time
can pass here without hurrying
it's a sharp blow which causes horror
not evanescence the sweet breath of nothing

Hic manebimus se vi piace non proprio
ottimamente ma il meglio sarebbe troppo simile
alla morte (e questa piace solo ai giovani)

[IL CREATORE FU INCREATO]

Il Creatore fu increato e questo
non mi tormenta. Se così non fosse
saremmo tutti ai suoi piedi
(si fa per dire)
infelici e adoranti.

[C'È UN SOLO MONDO ABITATO]

C'è un solo mondo abitato
da uomini
e questo è più che certo
un solo mondo, un globo in cui la caccia all'uomo
è lo sport in cui tutti sono d'accordo.
Non può essere un puro
fatto di malvagità
o il desiderio impellente
che infine il sole si spenga.
Ci sarà altro, ci sarà un perché
ma su questo gli dèi sono discordi.
Solo per questo hanno inventato il tempo,
lo spazio e una manciata di viventi.
Hanno bisogno di pensarci su

Hic manebimus if you like
not exactly in the best manner but
the best would be too much like death
(and only the young like that)

[THE CREATOR]

The Creator was uncreated and this
doesn't torment me. If
it were not so we would all be at his feet
(in a manner of speaking)
unhappy and adoring.

[THERE IS ONLY ONE WORLD]

There is only one world inhabited
by men
and this is more than certain
only one world, a globe where hunting men is
the sport all agree about.
It can't simply be a case of wickedness
or of the impelling desire that
the sun may at last be extinguished.
There must be something else, there may be
a why and a wherefore but
the gods don't agree about it.
That's why they have invented
time and space and a handful
of living beings. They have to think

perché se un accordo ci fosse
del loro crepuscolo non si parlerebbe più
e allora
poveri uomini senza dèi né demoni,
l'ultima, la peggiore delle infamie.

ASPASIA

A tarda notte gli uomini
entravano nella sua stanza
dalla finestra. Si era a pianterreno.
L'avevo chiamata Aspasia e n'era contenta.
Poi ci lasciò. Fu barista, parrucchiera e altro.
Raramente accadeva d'incontrarla.
Chiamavo allora Aspasia! a gran voce
e lei senza fermarsi sorrideva.
Eravamo coetanei, sarà morta da un pezzo.
Quando entrerò nell'inferno, quasi per abitudine
griderò Aspasia alla prima ombra che sorrida.
Lei tirerà di lungo naturalmente. Mai
sapremo chi fu e chi non fu
quella farfalla che aveva appena un nome
scelto da me.

UNA LETTERA CHE NON FU SPEDITA

Consenti mia dilettissima che si commendi
seppure con un lasso di più lustri
il mirifico lauro da te raccolto,

about it for if there were an agreement
one would no longer talk about their twilight
and then poor men without gods or demons,
the last, the worst of infamies.

ASPASIA

Late in the night
men used to enter her room
by the window. She lived on the ground floor.
I had named her Aspasia and she was pleased.
Then she left us. She worked as a barmaid,
a hairdresser and other things. It rarely happened
that I met her. But when I did,
I called out Aspasia! and she
would smile without stopping. We were
the same age, she must be long since dead.
When I enter Hell,
almost from force of habit I shall shout
Aspasia at the first shade that smiles.
Naturally she will keep on walking.
We shall never know who was and who wasn't
that butterfly who had just a name
chosen by me.

A LETTER THAT WASN'T SENT

Allow me my darling to commend
even though after a lapse of many lustrums
the marvelous laurel culled by you,

uno scavo di talpa neppure sospettabile
in chi era e sarà folgorata dal sole. Non importa
né a te né a me se accada che il tuo nome
resti nell'ombra. Il mondo può resistere
senza sfasciarsi solo se taluno
mantenga la promessa che gli estorse
con sorrisi e blandizie il Nume incognito
per cui vale la pena di vivere e morire.
Finito il turno si vedrà chi fosse
il vivente e chi il morto. Solo per questo
si può durare anche chiudendo gli occhi
per non vedere.

[SI RISOLVE BEN POCO]

Si risolve ben poco
con la mitraglia e col nerbo.
L'ipotesi che tutto sia un bisticcio,
uno scambio di sillabe è la più attendibile.
Non per nulla in principio era il Verbo.

TORPORE PRIMAVERILE

È tempo di rapimenti
si raccomanda di non uscire soli
le più pericolose sono le ore serali

with a mole-like digging one wouldn't
have suspected in one who was
and will be burnt up by the sun.
It makes no difference to you or to me
if your name should remain in the shade.
The world can hold out without collapsing
only if someone keeps the promise
extorted from him with smiles
and blandishments by the unknown God
for whom it's worth living and dying.
When one's turn is over we shall see
who the living were and who the dead.
For this alone can one
resist even as we close our eyes
so as not to see.

[ONE RESOLVES VERY LITTLE]

One resolves very little
with the machine gun or the whip.
The hypothesis that everything is a quibble,
a confusion of syllables is the most reliable.
Not for nothing in the beginning was the Word.

SPRING TORPOR

It's the time of kidnappings
one is advised not to go out alone
the evening hours are the most dangerous

ma evitate le diurne questo va da sé
i maestri di judo e di karaté
sono al settimo cielo
i sarti fanno gilets
a prova di pistola
i genitori dei figli vanno a scuola
i figli dei genitori ne fanno a meno
la nostra civiltà batte il suo pieno
scusate il francesismo rotte le museruole
le lingue sono sciolte non hanno freno.

[PROTEGGETEMI]

Proteggetemi
custodi miei silenziosi
perché il sole si raffredda
e l'ultima foglia dell'alloro
era polverosa
e non servì nemmeno per la casseruola
dell'arrosto —
proteggetemi da questa pellicola
da quattro soldi
che continua a svolgersi
davanti a me
e pretende di coinvolgermi
come attore o comparsa
non prevista dal copione —
proteggetemi persino
dalla vostra presenza
quasi sempre inutile

but avoid it goes without saying
the daytime ones too
the masters of judo and karate
are in the seventh heaven
the tailors make bulletproof vests
the parents of the children go to school
the children of the parents do without it
our civilisation is in full swing
excuse the Gallicism once
the muzzles are broken tongues are loosened
and there's no restraining them.

[PROTECT ME]

Protect me
my silent custodians
because the sun is turning cold
and the last leaf of the laurel
was dusty
and couldn't be used
even for the roast *en casserole*—
protect me from this
halfpenny film
which is being projected
before me
and presumes to involve me
as an actor or extra
not provided for by the script—
protect me even
from your own presence
almost always useless

e intempestiva
proteggetemi
dalle vostre spaventose assenze —
dal vuoto che create
attorno a me
proteggetemi dalle Muse
che vidi appollaiate
o anche dimezzate a mezzo busto
per nascondersi meglio
dal mio passo di fantasma —
proteggetemi o meglio ancora
ignoratemi
quando entrerò nel loculo
che ho già pagato da anni —
proteggetemi dalla fama/farsa
che mi ha introdotto nel Larousse illustrato
per scancellarmi poi
dalla nuova edizione —
proteggetemi
da chi impetra la vostra permanenza
attorno al mio catafalco —
proteggetemi con la vostra dimenticanza
se questo può servire a tenermi in piedi
poveri lari sempre chiusi nella vostra
dubbiosa identità —
proteggetemi senza che alcuno
ne sia informato
perché il sole si raffredda e chi lo sa
malvagiamente se ne rallegra
o miei piccoli numi
divinità di terz'ordine scacciate
dall'etere.

and inopportune
protect me
from your terrifying absences—
from the void which you create
around me
protect me from the Muses
whom I saw roosting
or reduced to their half busts
in order to hide better
from my ghost's step—
protect me or better still
ignore me
when I enter the urn
I have been paying for for years—
protect me from the fame/farce
which gained me entry into the illustrated Larousse
only to be omitted from
the new edition—
protect me
from those who beseech your presence
around my catafalque—
protect me with your forgetfulness
if it can help me keep on my feet
poor household gods always locked
in your dubious identity—
protect me without
anyone knowing about it
because the sun is turning cold
and he who knows it is
maliciously pleased
o my little gods
third-rate divinities
driven out of the ether.

HAMBURGER STEAK

Il tritacarne è già in atto ha blaterato
l'escatologo in furia; e poi a mezza voce
quasi per consolarci: speriamo che il suo taglio
non sia troppo affilato.

[I POETI DEFUNTI]

I poeti defunti dormono tranquilli
sotto i loro epitaffi
e hanno solo un sussulto d'indignazione
qualora un inutile scriba ricordi il loro nome.
Così accade anche ai fiori gettati nel pattume
se mai per avventura taluno li raccatti.
Erano in viaggio verso la loro madre
ora verso nessuno o verso un mazzo
legato da uno spago o da una carta argentata
e il cestino da presso senza nemmeno la gioia
di un bambino o di un pazzo.

PER FINIRE

In qualche parte del mondo
c'è chi mi ha chiesto un dito
e non l'ho mai saputo. La distanza
di quanto più s'accorcia di tanto si allontana.

HAMBURGER STEAK

The mincing machine is already in motion
babbled the escatologist in a fury; and then
in a lowered voice almost to console us:
let's hope its edge is not too sharp.

[THE DEAD POETS]

The dead poets sleep peacefully
under their epitaphs
and they only start with indignation
when a worthless writer
recalls their names.
And so do the flowers thrown into the rubbish heap
if someone should pick them up by chance.
They were on their way
to their mother but now
they are on their way to no one
or to a bunch held together by a string
or by silver paper and to the nearby garbage can
to the joy not even of a child or a madman.

TO FINISH

Somewhere in the world
there's one who asked me an inch
and I never knew it. The shorter
the distance becomes the farther it gets away.

DORMIVEGLIA

Il sonno tarda a venire
poi mi raggiungerà senza preavviso.
Fuori deve accadere qualche cosa
per dimostrarmi che il mondo esiste e che
i sedicenti vivi non sono tutti morti.
Gli acculturati, i poeti, i pazzi
le macchine gli affari le opinioni
quale nauseabonda olla podrida!
E io lì dento incrostato fino ai capelli!
Stavolta la pietà vince sul riso.

I RIPOSTIGLI

Non so dove io abbia nascosto la tua fotografia.
Fosse saltata fuori sarebbe stato un guaio.
Allora credevo che solo le donne avessero un'anima
e solo se erano belle, per gli uomini un vuoto
        assoluto.
Per tutti . . . oppure facevo un'eccezione per me?
Forse era vero a metà, ero un accendino
a corto di benzina. A volte qualche scintilla
ma era questione di un attimo.
L'istantanea non era di grande pregio:
un volto in primo piano, un arruffio di capelli.
Non si è saputo più nulla di te e neppure ho chiesto
possibili improbabili informazioni.
Oggi esiste soltanto il multiplo, il carnaio.

DROWSINESS

Sleep is slow to come
then it reaches me without warning.
Outside something must happen
to show me that the world exists
and that the self-styled living are not all dead.
Men of culture, poets, madmen
machines, business affairs, opinions
what a nauseating *olla podrida!*
And I within it encrusted
up to my eyes! This time
pity prevails over laughter.

THE HIDING PLACES

I don't know where I might have hidden
your photograph. Had it come to light
it would have been a nuisance.
At that time I believed that only
women had a soul and only
if they were beautiful,
for men an absolute void.
For all . . . or did I make an exception
of myself? Perhaps it was half true,
I was a lighter short of fluid.
Sometimes a spark but it was only
a question of a second.
The snapshot wasn't much good:
a close-up of your face, a tangle of hair.

137

Se vale il termitaio che senso ha la termite.
Ma intanto restava una nube, quella dei tuoi capelli
e quegli occhi innocenti che contenevano tutto
e anche di più, quello che non sapremo mai
noi uomini forniti di briquet,
di lumi no.

[OLTRE IL BREVE RECINTO DI FILDIFERRO]

Oltre il breve recinto di fildiferro
di uno di quei caselli ferroviari
dove fermano solo treni merci,
nello spazio in cui possono convivere
rosolacci e lattuga
c'era anche un pappagallo sul suo trespolo
e parlava parlava . . . ma dal mio omnibus
il tempo di ascoltarlo mi mancava.
Non è un ricordo di ieri, è di gioventù.
Mezzo secolo e più, ma non basta, non basta . . .

[DOPO I FILOSOFI]

Dopo i filosofi dell'omogeneo
vennero quelli dell'eterogeneo.
Comprendere la vita

One knew nothing more about you nor did I
ask for possible improbable information.
Today nothing exists but the multiple,
the carnage. If the termitary is valid,
what sense has the termite. But
in the meantime a cloud remained,
that of your hair and those innocent eyes
which contained everything and even more, some-
    thing
we shall never know, men furnished with lighters
but not with lights.

[BEYOND THE SMALL ENCLOSURE OF WROUGHT IRON]

Beyond the small enclosure of wrought iron
round one of those signalmen's cabins
where only freight trains stop,
and where poppies and lettuce can coexist
there was also a parrot on its trestle
and it talked and talked . . . but sitting
on my bus I didn't have time
to listen to it. Not a recent memory,
but one from my youth. More
than half a century ago,
but it's not enough, not enough . . .

[AFTER THE PHILOSOPHERS]

After the philosophers of the homogeneous
came those of the heterogeneous.
Only the mad could understand life

lo potevano solo i pazzi
ma a lampi e sprazzi
e ora non c'è più spazio
per la specola.
Solo qualche nubecola
qua e là
ma Dio ci guardi
anche da questa.

LOCUTA LUTETIA

Se il mondo va alla malora
non è solo colpa degli uomini
Così diceva una svampita
pipando una granita col chalumeau
al Café de Paris

Non so chi fosse A volte il Genio è quasi
una cosa da nulla, un colpo di tosse

LUNGOLAGO
Campione

Il piccolo falco pescatore
sfrecciò e finì in un vaso di terracotta
fra i tanti di un muretto del lungolago.
Nascosto nei garofani era visibile
quel poco da non rendere impossibile
un dialogo.

but by fits and starts
and now there's no longer any place
for the observatory.
Just some traces of cloud
here and there
but may God save us
even from these.

LOCUTA LUTETIA .

If the world is going to the dogs
it isn't only the fault of men
So said a gaunt old woman
sipping a crushed-ice drink through
a straw at the Café de Paris

I don't know who she was At times
Genius is almost a paltry thing,
a bout of coughing

BY THE LAKESIDE
Campione

The little fishhawk darted
and ended up in one of the many
terracotta vases on the wall
along the lakeside. Hidden amongst the carnations
just enough of it was visible to make
a dialogue possible.

Sei l'ultimo esemplare di una specie
che io credevo estinta, così dissi.
Ma la sovrabbondanza di voi uomini
sortirà eguale effetto mi fu risposto.
Ora apprendo osservai che si è troppi o nessuno.
Col privilegio vostro disse il falchetto
che qualcuno di voi vedrà il balletto finale.
A meno ribattei che tempo e spazio, fine
e principio non siano invenzioni umane
mentre tu col tuo becco hai divorato il Tutto.
Addio uomo, addio falco dimentica la tua pesca.
E tu scorda la tua senza becco e senz'ali,
omiciattolo, ometto.
                        E il furfante dispare in un alone
di porpora e di ruggine.

UN ERRORE

Inevitabilmente
diranno che qui parla un radoteur
come si misurasse col calendario
la saggezza.
Non esistono vite corte o lunghe
ma vite vere o vitemorte o simili.
Non sarò ripescato in qualche fiume
gonfio come una spugna. È un errore
che si paga.

You are the last example of a species
I believed to be extinct, I said.
But the superabundance of you men
will achieve the same result was the reply.
Now I realize I said that we are
too many or none. Thanks to your privilege
said the little fishhawk
some of you will see the final ballet.
Unless I countered time and space,
end and beginning are human inventions
while you with your beak have devoured Everything.
Good-bye man, good-bye fishhawk forget
your fishing. And you manikin little man
without beak or feathers forget yours.
                    And the rascal disappears
in a halo of purple and rust.

A MISTAKE

Inevitably
they will say that here speaks a dotard
as if wisdom could be measured
with a calendar.
There are no short or long lives but
real or dead ones or
something like that I shan't
be fished out of some river swollen
like a sponge. It's a mistake one has
to pay for.

[SPENTA L'IDENTITA]

Spenta l'identità
si può essere vivi
nella neutralità
della pigna svuotata dei pinòli
e ignara che l'attende il forno.
Attenderà forse giorno dopo giorno
senza sapere di essere se stessa.

I MIRAGGI

Non sempre o quasi mai la nostra identità personale
    coincide
col tempo misurabile dagli strumenti che abbiamo.
La sala è grande, ha fregi e stucchi barocchi
e la vetrata di fondo rivela un biondo parco di Stiria,
con qualche nebbiolina che il sole dissolve.
L'interno è puro Vermeer più piccolo e più vero
del vero ma di uno smalto incorruttibile.
A sinistra una bimba vestita da paggio
tutta trine e ricami fino al ginocchio
sta giocando col suo adorato scimmiotto.
A destra la sorella di lei maggiore, Arabella,
consulta una cartomante color di fumo
che le svela il suo prossimo futuro.
Sta per giungere l'uomo di nobile prosapia,
l'invincibile eroe ch'ella attendeva.
È questione di poco, di minuti, di attimi,
presto si sentirà lo zoccolìo dei suoi cavalli
e poi qualcuno busserà alla porta . . .

144

[ONCE IDENTITY IS EXTINGUISHED]

Once identity is extinguished
one can be alive in the neutrality of the pine cone
emptied of its seeds
and unaware that the furnace awaits it.
It will wait perhaps day after day
without knowing that it is itself.

THE MIRAGES

Our personal identity doesn't always
or almost never coincides with time
which can be measured with the instruments we
    have.
The hall is big, with baroque friezes and stuccos,
and the glass door at the bottom reveals
a blond Styrian park, with a few wisps of cloud
that the sun dissolves. The interior
is pure Vermeer smaller and more real
than the real one but of an incorruptible enamel.
On the left a little girl dressed as a page
all lace and embroidery down to the knee
is playing with her beloved monkey.
On the right her older sister, Arabella,
consults a smoke-colored crystal ball
which reveals her near future.
A nobleman is about to arrive,
the invincible hero she was waiting for.
It's a question of minutes, seconds,

qui il mio occhio si stanca e si distoglie
dal buco della serratura. Ho visto già troppo
e il nastro temporale si ravvolge in se stesso.
Chi ha operato il miracolo è una spugna di birra,
o tale parve, e il suo sodale è l'ultimo
Cavaliere di grazia della Cristianità.

. . . .

ma ora
se mi rileggo penso che solo l'inidentità
regge il mondo, lo crea e lo distrugge
per poi rifarlo sempre più spettrale
e inconoscibile. Resta lo spiraglio
del quasi fotografico pittore ad ammonirci
che se qualcosa fu non c'è distanza
tra il millennio e l'istante, tra chi apparve
e non apparve, tra chi visse e chi
non giunse al fuoco del suo cannocchiale. È poco
e forse è tutto.

MORGANA

Non so immaginare come la tua giovinezza
si sia prolungata

soon one will hear his horse's hoofs
and someone will knock at the door . . .

                                  but
at this point my eye tires and looks away
from the hole in the lock. I have already
seen too much and the temporal tape
winds up in itself.
He who worked the miracle is a soak,
or so he seemed, and his companion
the last Cavalier of grace of Christianity.

. . . .

but now
if I reread this I think
that only nonidentity supports the world,
creates and destroys it in order to
remake it increasingly more spectral
and inscrutable. There remains the small opening
of the almost photographic painter to admonish us
that if there was something there's no distance
between the millennium and the instant, between
who appeared and who didn't,
between him who lived and him
whom his telescope did not focus.
It isn't much and perhaps
it's everything.

MORGANA

I can't imagine how your youth
was prolonged so much (and how much!)

di tanto tempo (e quale!).
Mi avevano accusato
di abbandonare il branco
quasi ch'io mi sentissi
illustre, ex gregis o che diavolo altro.
Invece avevo detto soltanto revenons
à nos moutons (non pecore però)
ma la torma pensò
che la sventura di appartenere a un multiplo
fosse indizio di un'anima distorta
e di un cuore senza pietà.
Ahimè figlia adorata, vera mia
Regina della Notte, mia Cordelia,
mia Brunilde, mia rondine alle prime luci,
mia baby-sitter se il cervello vàgoli,
mia spada e scudo,
ahimè come si perdono le piste
tracciate al nostro passo
dai Mani che ci vegliarono, i più efferati
che mai fossero a guardia di due umani.
Hanno detto hanno scritto che ci mancò la fede.
Forse ne abbiamo avuto un surrogato.
La fede è un'altra. Così fu detto ma
non è detto che il detto sia sicuro.
Forse sarebbe bastata quella della Catastrofe,
ma non per te che uscivi per ritornarvi
dal grembo degli Dèi.

They had blamed me for having abandoned
the herd almost as if I felt
I was illustrious, *ex gregis* or
goodness knows what. In fact
all I had said was
revenons à nos moutons (not sheep
however) but the swarm thought
that the misfortune of belonging
to a multiple was the sign
of a distorted soul and
a pitiless heart. Alas
my adored daughter, my true
Queen of the Night, my Cordelia,
my Brunhilde, my swallow at dawn,
my baby-sitter if the mind should wander,
my sword and shield,
alas how one loses the track
chalked for us by the Manes
who watched over us,
the most ferocious that ever guarded
two human beings. They said
they wrote that we lacked faith.
Perhaps we had a substitute for it.
Faith is something else. They said
but what's said isn't necessarily right.
Perhaps faith in the Catastrophe would have been
enough, but not for you
who issued from the lap of the Gods
to return there.

NOTES TO THE POEMS

NOTES

Intellectual Education

The Guarantors: "the scientists, the positivists who believe in progress" (Montale).
the prince of the mad: Nietzsche who, in a fit of madness while in Turin, kissed the nose of a horse that was being flogged.

From the Lagoon

Erebus: the dark and gloomy cavern between earth and Hades.

Two Destinies

Celia: a reference to Celia Coplestone in T. S. Eliot's *The Cocktail Party.*

[Once]

David: Louis David (1748–1825), French neo-classical painter.

To Pio Rajna

Pio Rajna: Italian scholar and Professor of Romance philology (1847–1930).
Valtellina: in the province of Sondrio in Lombardy.
Inferno: the name of a red wine from Valtellina.

[When I Began to Paint]

my ant: reference to Montale's wife who is called Mosca, meaning a fly, in *Xenia*.
Piazza Navona: a famous square in the center of Rome.

Under a Lombard Painting

Palazzo Madama: in Rome, the meeting place of the Italian Senate of which Montale is an honorary member.
Cremona: Tranquillo Cremona (1837–1878), Italian painter.

The Talking Birds

the Indian birds: mynas.

The Sabià

The sabià: a Brazilian bird.

All Souls' Day

Gina: name of Montale's housekeeper.

[Life the Infinite Bubble]

Monti: Vincenzo Monti (1754–1828), Italian poet.

Honor

the land of gossip: Guido Piovene, Italian journalist, was born in Vincenza in Venetia, noted for its verbosity.

Heroism

Guadalajara: near Madrid, scene of a famous battle between General Franco's troops and the Republican troops.

Harmony

Adelheit: an imaginary name.

Disguises

Fregoli: Leopoldo Fregoli (1867–1936), a famous Italian quick-change artist; hence the word "fregolism," meaning sudden transformation.

Eulogy of our Times

well-known fable: the fable is by Aesop.

Soliloquy

Tristano: lyric drama in three acts by Wagner.
San Giorgio: Island of St. George in Venice which houses the famous cultural center, Cini Foundation.
famous pederast: J. J. Winckelmann (1717–1768), who was murdered in Trieste.

[Sub Tegmine Fagi]

Sub tegmini fagi: Virgil's phrase from *Bucolics,* Ecologue I: "*Tityre tu sub tegmine fagi*" (Tityrus, thou under the cover of the beech tree).

the cuttlefish bones: title of Montale's first book of poems, *Ossi di seppia*, which appeared in 1925.

[WE HAVE NOW REACHED]

Zebedee: an imaginary name.

LIVING

Villiers: Villiers de l'Isle-Adam (1838–1885), French novelist and dramatist, author of the dramatic poem, *Axël.*

THE PAPERWEIGHTS

"Buffalo" and *"Keepsake"*: poems from *Le occasioni.*
an eminent critic: Alfredo Gargiulo (1876–1949), who wrote a preface to Montale's *Ossi di seppia* and, later on, a review of *Le occasioni*. Montale is referring to the latter.

ON THE LAKE OF ORTA

The Lake of Orta is in Piedmont.

NOTES

Ahura Mazdah: divinity representing good in the Zoroastrian religion.
Ahriman: divinity representing evil in the Zoroastrian religion.

THE ELEPHANTS

a furtive tear: a reference to Donizetti's aria *"Una furtiva lacrima"* in *L'Elisir d'amore.*

CULTURE

Marcion: an early reformer of Christianity and founder of the Marcionite community.

Arius: philosopher and deacon of Alexandria and celebrated in ecclesiastical history. He lived during the reign of Constantine I.

IN A NORTHERN CITY

Marqués de Villanova: twentieth-century Spanish poet.

A DREAM, ONE OF MANY

Enrico the Scarecrow: An echo from Enrico Pea (1881–1958), Italian novelist and writer, whose novel *Moscardino* Ezra Pound translated into English. Pea says in *Moscardino: si scorge già il bianco sul cariolino di legno,* ("one can already see the white of the wood on the spool").

THE DISAPPEARANCE OF THE SCREECH OWLS

A son of Minerva: the owl which is sacred to the goddess Minerva.

FROM THE OTHER BANK

Gerti: A character in Montale's earlier poem, "Carnevale di Gerti," in *Le occasioni.*

the two-headed eagle: the insignia of the Austro-Hungarian Empire.

On the Beach

Cavalca: Domenica Cavalca (1270–1342), a Dominican and author of *Vita dei Santi Padri;* a prose writer favored by the Vocabolario della Crusca.

Spring Torpor

Gallicism: "is in full swing" or *battere il suo pieno* is a translation of the French idiom *battre son plein.*

Drowsiness

This time pity prevails over laughter: reference to Leopardi. After considering (in *La ginestra*) man's pathetically helpless and precarious position in the universe and at the same time his fatuous claim to be both the center and the *raison d'être* of the universe, Leopardi doesn't know what to feel for him and observes: *Non so se il riso o la pietà prevale* ("I don't know whether laughter or pity prevails").

Locuta Lutetia

Locuta Lutetia: Parisian talk.

By the Lakeside

Campione: an Italian town in Swiss territory, near Lake Lugano.

INDEX/ITALIAN

INDEX OF TITLES AND FIRST LINES/ITALIAN

INDEX/ENGLISH

INDEX OF TITLES AND FIRST LINES/ENGLISH

Some New Directions Paperbooks

For complete listing request complete catalog from
New Directions, 80 Eighth Avenue, New York 10011   † Bilingual